SMALL PET
HANDBOOK

TO BETTY AND ELIZABETH

First published in 1996 by
HarperCollins*Publishers*
London

© HarperCollins*Publishers* Ltd 1996

First U.S. edition published in 1997 by
Barron's Educational Series, Inc.

David Taylor asserts the moral right to be identified as the author of this work.

All inquiries should be addressed to:
Barron's Educational Series, Inc.
250 Wireless Boulevard
Hauppauge, NY 11788

International Standard Book No. 0-7641-5033-2

Library of Congress Catalog Card No. 96-29778

Library of Congress Cataloging-in-Publication Data
Taylor, David, 1934-
     Small pet handbook / David Taylor.
         p.   cm.
     Includes index.
     ISBN 0-7641-5033-2
     1. Rabbits. 2. Rodents as pets.   I. Title
    SF453.T29   1997
    636.9'322–dc21   96-29778
                              CIP

This book was created by SP Creative Design for HarperCollins*Publishers* Ltd
Editor: Heather Thomas
Designer: Rolando Ugolini
Illustrations: Al Rockall, Rolando Ugolini
Special photography: Animal Ark and Rolando Ugolini
Frank Lane Picture Agency: pages 8, 17, 80, 82, 84, 91, 93, 94
David Dalton: pages 66, 70

Colour reproduction by Colourscan, Singapore
Printed and bound by New Interlitho SpA, Italy

987654321

BARRON'S
SMALL PET
HANDBOOK

Consulting Editor
Petra Burgmann DVM

DAVID TAYLOR
BVM&S, FRCVS, FZS

Author

David Taylor, BVMS, FRCVS, FZS, is a well-known veterinary surgeon, broadcaster, and author of over 30 books, including six volumes of autobiography, some of which formed the basis for three series of the BBC television drama *One by One*. The founder of the International Zoo Veterinary Group, he has exotic patients across the world, ranging from crocodiles to killer whales and giant pandas. He lives in Richmond, Surrey, with his wife, four cats, and a hamster called "Fudge."

Contents

Introduction

Small, as they say, is beautiful. That's certainly true of the small pets that are ideal for young people who are beginning to revel in the joys and responsibilities of animal keeping because they are relatively inexpensive to buy and maintain. However, they are also a fascinating hobby for innumerable adults. It is estimated that there are about 4.2 million rabbits, 3.4 million hamsters, and 1.7 million guinea pigs in the United States at the present time, as well as roughly 2 million tame rats, mice, and gerbils. Indeed, rabbits are the third most common pet examined by veterinarians in their hospitals.

Although these small mammals generally cost less than dogs and cats, not to mention ponies and horses, they deserve and demand no less care and attention from their owners in order to ensure them long and happy lives. Such intriguing creatures are not to be regarded as children's toys, or disposable, second-rate pets. Housed and handled properly, and tended and treated with affection and interest, these little animals, which come in such a wide variety of breeds and colors, will provide limitless fascination, fun, and, yes, friendship.

All of them are designed and constructed as intricately as dogs, horses, or, indeed, human beings. Their delicate, complex anatomy and physiology, perfectly attuned to a particular mode of living on this planet, make man-made devices such as computers and space rockets seem Stone Age by comparison. What's more, from a practical point of view, they are healthier to have around than, say, dogs or cats. Rabbits and rats and all the other small pets, in their domesticated forms, carry fewer diseases that can be transmitted to their owners than the bigger species.

To get the most out of your small pet means putting in a little effort to learn the do's and don'ts, the basic rules for maintaining them correctly. It isn't at all difficult as this little book will show you, and the more you learn about, observe, and work with your pets, the more your enjoyment and delight will grow in these very special animals.

CHAPTER ONE

Rabbits

The name "rabbit" probably comes from a medieval Dutch word "robbe," which was originally a nickname for anyone called Robert.

■ Evolution of the rabbit

Rabbits are not rodents like rats, mice, and other pets featured in this book, but are members of another group of mammals called lagomorphs. These creatures originated around 55,000,000 years ago and developed quite separately from the rodents. One key difference between rodents and lagomorphs is that, whereas the former have only one pair of upper incisor (gnawing) teeth, the latter have two pairs. Modern scientific blood analysis shows the lagomorphs to be

These hares are "boxing" in the mating season.

more closely related to hoofed animals than to rodents. There are
three main groups of lagomorphs:

- Rabbits
- Hares
- Pikas

The last group, the pikas, is the least familiar to most of us. They
are small (0.125–0.3 m/7–12 in long), with rounded ears, short legs,
and virtually no tail. The only European species live in Russia. They
are hardy creatures of the mountains and one, the Tibetan pika,
can be found lying out in the Himalayan sun at altitudes above
5,500 m/18,000 ft and in temperatures of –15°C/5°F or less. The
differences between rabbits and hares are outlined on page 10.

■ Rabbits in Britain

It is generally thought that rabbits were introduced into Britain
no earlier than 1066 when the Normans invaded. They brought
"warreners" with them – men who would stock and tend rabbit
warrens to supply the invaders' stomachs.

However, there is evidence that rabbits may have reached Britain
before the Normans. Fossilized remains record their presence before
the third Glacial Age (22,000 years ago). It is certain that they
didn't survive the icy conditions. After the ice receded, Europe and
North Africa were repopulated with rabbits moving out from the
Iberian Peninsula. Some scientists believe that rabbits may then
have crossed the land bridge between France and Britain around
7000–6000 BC; England was connected to the Continent up to
about 5000 BC. It is also possible that the Romans, hearty eaters
who had domesticated rabbits by the first century BC and kept them
in special walled enclosures called *leporia,* may have introduced
some of these animals.

Rabbit soon became a choice meat on medieval menus, and their
fur and skins were in demand. Rabbit embryos were considered
meatless and an acceptable food for fast days. By the fourteenth

Rabbits and hares

	Rabbits	Hares
At birth	Born naked, blind, and helpless	Born well covered with fur and hop about shortly after birth
Nature	Generally gregarious	Generally solitary
Habitat	Usually in burrows	Usually above ground
Running	Scamper, no stamina	Excellent runners, good staying power

The best-selling book *Watership Down* helped to increase interest in rabbits and keeping them as pets.

century, rabbit was valued as highly as suckling pig. As agriculture evolved and natural predators, such as falcons and wild carnivores, diminished, rabbits became more of a problem to the farmers' crops. Trapping, snaring, and ferreting continued with rabbits still popular for food and the furrier trade, but with three rabbits eating as much each day as one sheep, the loss of arable produce was significant by the nineteenth century.

Sending ferrets down the burrows to do battle with the rabbits underground had always been the most popular method of control, but all sorts of bizarre methods were tried to rid fields of the free-loading rabbits. Most interesting of all is the way in which farmers on the Isle of Wight fixed lighted candles to the backs of crabs and sent them down burrows, presumably to terrorize the rabbits into living elsewhere. Crabs and lobsters were similarly employed in Devon and were known as "sea ferrets." And while all this was going on, gypsies in the Chilterns claimed to be getting even better results with "ferreting" toads!

■ Species of rabbit

Wild rabbits occur in most but not all parts of the world. They are absent from Scandinavia, the Balkans, Italy, and Eastern Europe. There are 25 species of wild rabbit worldwide, living in a variety of habitats from the dense vegetation on the slopes of volcanoes (the volcano rabbit) to bogs and swamps (the marsh rabbit and swamp rabbit).

Only one Old World rabbit species exists: *Oryctolagus*. It covers much of Europe and North Africa, was introduced into Australia and New Zealand and elsewhere by settlers, and is the origin of all domestic rabbit breeds. Among the other 24 species is the dark-colored Pentalagus, found only on the Ryukyu Islands of Japan, and

These handsome animals are English rabbits, a breed that originated in the nineteenth century.

Names for rabbits

Country people had quaint names for different wild rabbits.
- Warreners lived in established warrens.
- Parkers were to be found in open country.
- Hedgehogs were those in thickly wooded areas or alternatively in no fixed area.
- Sweethearts were rabbits bred in captivity. Sweethearts of the eighteenth and nineteenth centuries were usually kept in pits and were fed on brewery grain, cabbage leaves, turnip tops, and other vegetable refuse. Gradually, the selective breeding of the rabbit developed and by 1880 the keeping of rabbits as pets began to be very popular.

the incredibly rare Nesolagus from Sumatra. This small rabbit with short ears and a mottled coat may already be extinct, as only 13 specimens have ever been found!

■ European rabbits

The single species of European wild rabbit was and is found in a variety of different natural types. Albinos are rare, but a Dutch marked variety with a white nose and saddle mark is not uncommon. A long-haired Angora type lives on the Welsh islands of Skomer and Skokholm but rarely elsewhere, and melanistic (black) ones form almost 100 percent of the communities on the British Scilly Isles and the Islet of Samson.

By crossing and selecting from the fast and prolifically breeding animal, man produced the 50-odd breeds and around 80 varieties of the modern rabbit fancy. You can choose from a wide range of sizes, coat colors, designs, and textures. With the glamorous varieties of domesticated pet rabbit now available, we are a long way from *Watership Down*.

■ Domesticated rabbits

There are four main groups of domesticated rabbit:

■ Normal fur

These include Chinchilla, Havana, New Zealand, Sable, Smoke Pearl, Fox, Lilac, and Chinchilla giganta. Some Normal Furs, such as the Squirrel, Glavcot, and Perle de Hal, are now extinct. The breeds come in a variety of elegant colors.

■ Rex

These breeds have a plush coat, about 1.25 cm/$^1/_2$ in long and with a velvety touch. They include the Self, Shaded, and Tan. Again, there are lots of named color varieties.

■ Satins

Here the fur is shiny to the touch due to each hair being flattened and with little or no hollow center. The breeds of Satin come

There are many breeds of rabbit, and they come in a wide range of colors and sizes, such as the Dutch rabbits (top) and Old English (above), which are among the fancy breeds.

Coneys

Incidentally, the coney mentioned in the Bible is not the rabbit. The word "coney" does indeed come from the Latin for rabbit and it is still used to mean rabbit in heraldry and the fur trade. Many dictionaries and biblical scholars confuse the two words, but the conies that "are but a feeble folk, yet make they their houses in the rocks" (Proverbs) refers to a totally different rodent-like creature (actually the closest living relative of the elephant) called the Syrian hyrax, which lives in Palestine.

in a broad spectrum of colors with names like Argent, Fox, Himalayan, Ivory, Lilac, Marten Sable, Opal, and Smoke Pearl.

■ Fancy breeds

These include the Angora, Belgian Hare, Dutch, English, Harlequin Magpie, Himalayan, Lop, Netherland Dwarf, Polish, Silver, and Tan. **Note:** There are well-known breeds like that schoolchildren's favorite, the Dutch, and real rarities such as the Orange-buff Shaded Rex and the Smoke Pearl Marten Rex. No rabbit could be humble with a name like this.

■ Weight

Lagomorphs range in weight from 100 grams/$3^1/2$ oz for the smallest pikas up to around 4.6 kg/over 10 lb for the largest wild hares. Domestic breeds of rabbit can exceed that with weights of 5.5–6.3 kg/12–$13^3/4$ lb, generally in adult Flemish Giants; the record is 11.3 kg/almost 25 lb, achieved by both a Flemish Giant and a Norfolk Star. It must be admitted, however, that rabbits are not particularly efficient users of food. The rate at which they extract available energy from food is only about one-third of that achieved by sheep or cows. However, they are more damp-resistant than sheep, and they have survived in wet, chilly environments that have wiped out sheep flocks.

■ Voice

Rabbits are not usually very noisy creatures. They are generally non-vocal unless injured or frightened, although some do give little grunts of pleasure. One species, the South African red "hare" (*Pronolagus*), emits a high-pitched warning call when trouble is brewing.

■ Speed

Unlike the hare, which can clock up to 80 kmph/50 mph, the rabbit is not a very fast runner. It dashes and scampers and seeks the safety of a burrow rather than trying to outrun a pursuer. It is, however,

quite an accomplished swimmer, and the marsh and swamp rabbits (*Sylvilagus* species) of the Americas and the West Indies take to water with gay abandon. Surprisingly, rabbits also climb well and can be found living in the thatched roofs of cottages in the Hebrides. The rabbit's foot has hair on the undersurface to afford a good grip.

■ Vision

Rabbits possess good eyesight but are color-blind. The most impressive aspect is their range of vision. With eyes set well out on both sides of the head, they cover a field of over 300°; they can literally see behind them. The eyes can move in conjunction or independently of each other. Because of the position of their eyes, rabbits do not see stereoscopically, as do humans and monkeys for example, but to hunted animals stereoscopic vision is less important than all-around warning capability.

Other creatures that usually find themselves playing the part of innocent victims, such as the mouse, shrew, and partridge, also have eyes set to the sides like the rabbit. The problem is the area in front of the nose, particularly the nearest 2 m/6 ft, which is poorly seen by the rabbit or hare. To overcome this difficulty, it has to tip its head a little to one side so that one eye at a time can scan the awkward zone.

The position of the eyes explains why, when a hare is pursued by a dog, it lifts its head up and lays its ears back; it can see the dog behind. But it has that blind spot dead ahead and in full flight there's no time to waste tipping one's head to the right or left. Consequently, hares sometimes dash headlong over a cliff or straight into a pair of human legs.

There is no shimmering, reflecting mirror behind the retina of a rabbit as seen in a hunter, such as the cat. The red color of an albino's eyes is simply the layer of blood vessels behind the retina. There is also, however, an intriguing dull eyeshine frequently seen in rabbits; scientists do not understand how this is produced. The retina, the light-sensitive film of the eye, is much more highly organized and complex in rabbits than in man or other primates. Whereas the rabbit sorts out and interprets in the retina itself much of the visual information coming into the eye, higher creatures, such as primates, have shifted such functions back into the more sophisticated sight-control areas of the brain. The poor rabbit needs what little brain it has for other things.

■ Smell

Rabbits are excellent sniffers; they're so good that they go hunting the elusive underground truffle fungus by scent alone. All that nose-twitching of rabbits and hares is probably linked with smell, but there

Scent

This is very important to rabbits. Males use odors to mark their territory and their possessions. They do this either by spraying urine (with considerable accuracy and range) or by transferring

a special substance from glands under their chins onto their paws and then stamping it along their boundary lines or rubbing it on to females and young belonging to them. Chin-scratching in rabbits denotes male chauvinism rather than an irritating itch.

may be some additional sensory function extracting information from the air. Beneath the twitching folds of skin but in front of the nostrils are two hairless patches of skin in the form of oval, raised pads covered with pimples and ridges. What do they detect? How do they work? Science has yet to find out. Rabbits are by no means smelly creatures. Young rabbits are remarkably free of scent and necessarily so in a world of keen-nosed predators. A fox, which can locate eggs buried 10 cm/4 in deep when passing by at a distance of 2.7 m/3 yd, normally misses baby rabbits buried in sand by their mother while she goes out searching for food.

■ Hearing and taste

Rabbits come fully equipped with other highly developed senses. Hearing is first-class with long, mobile ear flaps that can swivel around to scoop faint sounds out of the air. As befits such a vegetarian epicure, the rabbit appears to enjoy a sense of taste that is likewise one of the best around. The rabbit mouth possesses 17,000 taste buds compared with only 10,000 in humans, only 400 in parrots, and a minute 30–60 in pigeons.

■ Teeth and digestion

Rabbit teeth are not at all like ours or those of the dog or cat. They keep on growing continually throughout life, pushing continually up out of the gum and being worn down to convenient size by chewing.

Rabbit bowels are notable mainly for the presence of a well-developed large intestine where the fibrous vegetable food is acted

Touch

As with other animals with whiskers, the rabbit uses these sensitive touch-antennae, particularly at night. The whiskers also feel for the walls of the familiar dark tunnels under the ground, and the feel of the home burrow is registered in the kinesthetic (touch) memory section of the brain. Put a rabbit in a strange burrow and the alarm bells begin ringing in this programmed memory bank; under such conditions a rabbit is likely to panic. So unpleasant is the idea of a foreign burrow to a rabbit that it will usually seek any refuge (bushes, reeds, etc.), even with a hunter hot on its heels, rather than use a handy foreign hole.

on by the population of digestive microbes. This microbial digestion is similar to what happens in the stomachs of cud-chewing animals, such as cows, and when the germs have done their work the contents of the intestine are much richer in useful nourishment. Unfortunately, quite a lot of this potentially useful digested food passes out of the body in the droppings. Very sensibly, the rabbit, true to the maxim "waste not, want not," eats these droppings and thereby gets the benefit of the vitamins and other goodies that it nearly lost. This dropping-eating process is called coprophagia. It applies only to softer, light-colored stools (caecotrophs), which in wild rabbits are usually

passed when they are resting in their burrows. The darker, drier droppings passed when the rabbit is out and about contain much less nourishment and are not eaten.

The two types of dropping are easily recognized in domestic rabbits, although some pets are so quick at eating the caecotrophs that you may miss seeing them. Rabbits and hares, of course, are not ruminants like cattle, sheep, deer, and antelopes; they don't chew cud.

■ Fur

Every rabbit comes with an excellent fur coat that is composed in most breeds of long guard hairs and undercoat. Molting takes place normally once a year and spreads backwards from the front of the shoulders, over the flanks, and ends finally with the underbelly. The guard hairs are absent in Rex rabbits but luxuriously long in Angoras.

■ Coat color and lifespan

Some domestic rabbits produce different coat colors depending upon the temperature at which they are kept. Himalayans, for example, are pure white in an environment above 28°C/84°F.

These white Lops have a soft coat with long guard hairs.

At lower temperatures, they show black paws, black tips to the ears, and black saddlemarks. The low temperatures for some reason stimulate the production of black pigment cells in the skin while the hair is growing. The rabbit's lifespan is normally six to eight years.

This Old English rabbit has a distinctive coat.

CHAPTER TWO

Rodents

Apart from the rabbit, the other small pets in this book are all rodents. Rodents, which are characterized by having one pair of upper and one pair of lower incisor teeth designed for gnawing, are the most numerous of all mammals (50 percent of all species of mammal fall into the Order *Rodentia*).

■ Size

They range in size from the Old World harvest mouse, which can weigh as little as 4.2 grams/one-seventh of an ounce, up to the South American capybara, which tips the scales at 30–50 kg/ 65–110 lb. Fossil rodents as big as wild boar and with heads the size of bulls have been discovered in Uruguay.

Guinea pigs (or cavies)

All of these mini-pets, as we have noted, are equipped with nipping incisor teeth, and a hamster, if provoked or neglected, can bite painfully. Yet none is more gentle and uncomplaining than our next subject, the cavy, commonly called the guinea pig.

Where does the strange name come from? The animal itself originated in South America, where wild relatives are still to be found in Peru. Some guinea pigs live at very high altitudes in the mountains. Scarcity of meat animals in the Andes led the pre-Inca natives to domesticate the guinea pig. Indeed, for centuries it was the only domesticated food animal of Peru, and it was also used as a sacrifice to the gods. Guinea pigs began to spread out of the Inca empire following the Spanish conquests of the mid-sixteenth century, and arrived in Europe via West Africa (by way of Guinea, perhaps?) in the seventeenth century. However, the word "Guinea" may not have

The English guinea pig is the most popular variety.

In the wild

Whatever the origin of these animals' odd name, they are admirable individuals. In the wild, they live peaceably in burrows, wander around in the daytime and at night, being neither strictly nocturnal nor strictly diurnal, eat a purely vegetarian diet, and converse with one another in faint squeaks and grunts.

any geographical significance. In the seventeenth and eighteenth centuries it meant foreign or strange.

■ Varieties

There are three main varieties of domestic guinea pig:
- The English (most common)
- The Abyssinian
- The Peruvian (least common)

■ **The English variety** is short-haired and comes in self-colored types (cream, black, white, agouti, etc.) or as mixtures of two colors (bicolors) or three colors (tricolors). Color patterns similar to those in rabbits are given the same names (such as Himalayan, Dutch, etc.).

■ **Abyssinians** are also short-coated but the coat is rougher and arranged in whorls and rosettes. This variety also comes in many different colors.

■ **The Peruvian** is long-haired (hairs up to 2 cm/³/₄ in long) and again is to be found in various colors.

■ Vision and lifespan

Unlike hamsters, and most other rodents, guinea pigs do have some degree of color vision. Their average lifespan is four to eight years.

■ Teeth – gnawing and chewing

Guinea pigs are typical rodents. They have the four characteristic, chisel-like incisor teeth, which continue to grow throughout the entire lifetime of the animal. When gnawing, there is a forward and backward movement of the lower incisors that bite against the upper pair. While this is going on, the grinding cheek teeth or molars do not meet one another, and indeed the back of the mouth can be shut off by pulling in the cheeks behind the incisors. This mechanism allows gnawing to proceed for some time without swallowing gnawed material and saves wear on the molars. When the guinea pig decides to change from gnawing to chewing, the lower jaw moves backward, one set of incisors fits neatly behind the other, and the molars come into contact to begin the grinding process prior to swallowing. All this fancy mouthwork is controlled by a complicated set of special muscles.

Digestion

Again, like other rodents, guinea pigs possess a large cecum, a cul-de-sac lying at the junction between the small and large intestines where vegetable matter (often full of cellulose and tough to break down) can spend some time for digestion to be completely effective.

Hamsters

These sturdy Old World rodents include such species as the tiny
Chinese hamster and the European or black-bellied hamster, as well
as the golden hamster, the most common one found in pet stores. In
the wild, these solitary animals live in burrows and feed on fruit,
grain, and vegetables. Some species eat insects and other small
creatures. All hamsters possess cheek pouches into which they can
pack food, and hence their name, which comes from German, where
"hamster" means "hoarder."

■ Color, weight, and sight

Over 30 color varieties of golden hamster have been produced by
selective breeding. These include cream, cinnamon, white sepia,
honey, silver-blue and dark, normal, and light golden. They can be

Golden hamsters

The golden hamster is sometimes called the Syrian hamster
although, in fact, the species is not confined to Syria but is
native to the plains of Asia Minor and the Balkans. Every single
hamster in captivity today is descended from a single family of
golden hamsters that was captured in Syria by Dr. Aharoni in
1932. They were taken to the Hebrew University of Jerusalem
and were found to thrive well. The family consisted of a female
and seven young. Four escaped and one female was killed by a
male. That left one male and two females. These three animals
formed the ancestral stock of almost every golden hamster that
has ever been kept in a laboratory or a youngster's bedroom
despite a further introduction of wild stock made in 1971. They
bred well and were first exported to the United States in 1938.
So much for the dangers of inbreeding!

banded. There are also piebalds, mosaics, satinized, and tortoiseshells. Their eyes may be black or red in color.

The basic golden hamster is reddish-brown in color with white underparts, measures 15-20 cm/6-8 in long and weighs 85-130 g/ 3-5 oz. It is color-blind and sees the world in black and white.

■ Development and activity

Anatomically, hamsters are constructed to a design that is basically the same as that of the rabbit or mouse. Biologically, the most striking thing about them is their remarkably rapid rate of development. A hamster takes only 60 days to proceed from being a single egg cell in its mother's uterus to becoming a parent itself.

Hamsters are mainly active in the darker hours, particularly between 8 and 11 PM, and if the dark and light periods of the day are reversed artificially, they adjust their activity to the times when the lights are low. During their daily busy time, they may regularly travel between 11 and 21 km/6.8–13 miles. In captivity, their energy is directed particularly toward escaping, and females in heat generally show an ingenious determination to go "absent without leave." Hamsters are very fastidious animals much given to grooming, especially after being touched by human hands. Their normal life expectancy is one to three years.

Regular gentle handling is good for hamsters.

Gerbils

The friendly, inquisitive gerbil, with its brownish (agouti) fur and large dark eyes, is a very popular pet. The usual species found in a pet store is the Mongolian gerbil, but sometimes you will come across the Libyan kind. In fact, over 80 species of gerbil exist, and they differ widely in size, color, length of tail, and even the color of their toenails. Pet gerbils have now been bred in other colors besides brown. There are also albinos, blacks, and piebalds.

■ In the wild

Gerbils are rodents that are particularly adapted to living in arid environments; they are found in the wild in the deserts and plains of Africa and Asia, and from the southwest of Russia in the west to the north of China in the east.

Most gerbils spend their days in underground burrows where the temperature is constant at about 20–25°C/68–79°F, sometimes blocking the entrance to their hiding place with a stone or lump of earth. High temperatures can be quickly lethal to these little animals and most species are nocturnal, venturing out to forage for food in the cool of the night. Mongolian and Great gerbils of the colder, northern lands are among the few species that are active by day and night.

■ Digestion

Obtaining and conserving water is crucially important to gerbils. They obtain some by "burning" the carbohydrates in the seeds and other vegetable matter that they eat, but they also collect such food when it is damp with dew. Their digestive system extracts water from the food with great efficiency, allowing them to pass very dry droppings, and their powerful kidneys retain as much water as possible so that they produce only a few drops of very concentrated urine.

Although most gerbils are herbivorous, they will eat almost anything else they find. One species, Wagner's gerbil, has a passion for snails.

Pet gerbils

Pet gerbils tame quickly, seldom bite, and have a life expectancy of around five years. Good jumpers, they nevertheless have no idea of heights and so should not be left alone on a table as they may leap off and injure themselves.

Survival in the wild

Gerbils' bodies are modified specially in ways that aid survival when predators are near.

■ They possess very large middle ears enabling them to detect the soft wing beats of owls.

■ Their eyes are set so as to provide a wide field of vision.

■ For camouflage, their coat colors are the same as that of the terrain on and in which they live. Even within the same species, gerbils living among dark brown volcanic rocks develop dark brown fur while those living in orange sand have orange fur.

■ The long tail acts as a stabilizer when jumping and as a support when standing on the hind legs to look around.

The pale-colored underparts of the gerbil reflect heat from the hot ground of the desert and thus help cool the animal.

Mice and rats

Now we come to the smallest and most inexpensive subjects of this book, traditionally beloved by small boys and looked at askance by most elderly people above the age of 15. Small they may be and easy on the pocket (and in the pocket of many a young enthusiast), but they are pieces of biological engineering as intricate and intriguing as any of the more sophisticated pets.

Lively, easily tamed, loving little individuals, tame breeds of rat are clean, gentle, fascinating creatures that carry less risk of disease for their owners than domestic dogs. They bond with humans more easily than any other kind of small pet, and tame mice are neither Robert Burn's "wee sleekit, cow'rin', tim'rous beasties" nor voracious little demons.

■ Varieties of mouse

As a group, mice are a varied and enterprising bunch and are by no means limited to holes in baseboards, lumps of cheese, and sinking ships. There are the birch mice of Eurasia that leap rather than run, live in burrows, and sensibly hibernate in the bitter winters of the plains; the grasshopper mice of North America that share burrows with prairie dogs and are useful in controlling insects, their favorite food, and sometimes kill birds or other rodents; the jumping mice with gray, golden, or yellow-brown fur, long hind legs, and very long tails, some of which live in America while other little-known ones roam the Giant Panda forests of China; and the spiny pocket mice of the Mexican deserts with their harsh fur.

Species of mice and rats

There are dozens of different wild mouse and rat species, and the domesticated ones come in a wide variety of colors and patterns, not just plain white. Both rats and mice can be bicolored. Hooded rats are bicolored with one of the colors covering the head and shoulders to resemble a hood.

Russia has the delicate Selevin's mouse, a corpulent little fellow only discovered in 1939. It loves to eat spiders and is very nocturnal; in fact, it can't take more than a few minutes of sunshine without becoming ill! Between Alaska and the tip of South America live over 60 species of deer mice, pretty creatures with big eyes, fur that can range in color from white through brown to black but always with dappled white feet. In Australia, sure enough, there's a mouse with a

pouch, the marsupial mouse, which is not a true mouse at all but a diminutive relative of the kangaroo. These are just a few of the many different species in existence.

■ Types of rat

What is the difference between a rat and a mouse? Not an easy question – it isn't a matter of size for there are small species of rat and large species of mouse. To scientists, rats and mice are simply names given to various species within the animal family Muridae. Rats have more rows of scales on their tails (210 or more) than do mice (never more than 180).

Apart from the notorious brown rat and the black rat, there are water rats with large, laterally compressed tails that are used for sculling, swamp rats, tree rats, field rats, jerboa rats, bamboo rats, and kangaroo rats, to name but a few. Jerboa rats have long hind limbs and tufted tails and are found in North Australia. Africa has giant rats measuring 74 cm/$2^1/2$ ft in total length, the spiny tree rat with its spiny coat, and Rhabdomys, the field rat with four stripes. In the Solomon Islands you will find a woolly rat, Capromys, whereas New Guinea is the home of Mallomys, a very large species with gorgeous long hair speckled with white, and Anisomys, which is coarse-haired and creamy-colored all over except for a dark base to its tail. The rarest rodent in the world is probably Swarth's rice rat. Only four have ever been seen alive (in 1906), and it wasn't recorded again until 1966 when the skull of a recently deceased animal was found. The home of this elusive creature, if it still exists, is on James Island in the Galapagos.

Our elegant, well-bred tame rats might well frown on the black sheep of the rodent family, their infamous cousins the wild black and brown rats. There are estimated to be around a hundred million of these two species in the United States, and each animal costs the country hundreds of millions of dollars per year in crop spoilage alone.

■ Life expectancy and sight

The life expectancy of the average rat or mouse in the wild is generally short and can be reckoned in weeks or months. Pet mice, however, will reach three years of age and sometimes five years. They have built in (possibly truly magnetic) homing instincts but are almost certainly color blind, viewing their world in black and white.

■ Water requirements

Like most rodents, mice and rats need to take in little water; they produce almost all they require under normal circumstances by burning the carbohydrates in the food they eat and using the water

Adaptation to environment

Being versatile and generally not over-specialized, rats and mice have successfully adapted to nearly every environment the earth has to offer. For example, house mice sometimes live inside the insulating material within refrigerator walls and adapt to the chillier lifestyle by growing longer hair.

that is released in their bodies as a by-product of the burning. This metabolic water is produced by larger animals, including humans, but to them it is a minor source of H_2O; their relatively massive bodies demand far more water than such an internal spring can supply. Desert species, such as the spiny mouse, like the gerbils, can survive happily without any external source of water. As an extra water conservation measure, such species produce only limited amounts of droppings and highly concentrated urine. Some spiny mice can live purely on tiny quantities of seawater and even your ordinary house mouse can get by almost indefinitely without liquids. However, this does not mean that you should ever leave your tame rats and mice without a source of fresh, clean water! They are domesticated varieties that, particularly in the case of rats, may not be as hardy as their wild cousins.

Agility and movement

Some species, such as the kangaroo rats and jumping mice, are excellent jumpers; they have very enlarged tympanic bullae (the bony covering of the middle ear) that are concerned with balancing and also, possibly, with improving hearing in the desert where these creatures live.

South American fish-eating rats and water rats are naturally first-class swimmers. Some are skilled climbers, like the tree rats and tree mice. The wild black rat is a fine climber, being originally a tree-dweller, and it can dash along telephone wires more nimbly than any tightrope walker. Although many naturalists believe that the brown rat cannot climb, this is untrue; it is not as agile as its black rat relative but it can clamber up things quite proficiently.

CHAPTER THREE

Acquiring your pet

So you think a pet rabbit, guinea pig, hamster, gerbil, rat, or mouse is just the thing for you. But wait, are you just the thing for a pet? Before taking on the responsibility of owning any sort of living, breathing, feeling creature, there are some points that you should consider carefully. Ask yourself the following questions and answer them honestly.

1 Are you committed enough to look after the animal or animals for 365 days a year, not just for the first week or two before the novelty wears off?

2 What about vacations – what then?

3 Do you know about the animals' needs for housing, exercise, feeding, etc.?

4 Will you be able to provide enough space for animals that love company like rabbits and guinea pigs?

5 Do you know whether they smell and can you, day in, day out, combat all odors by regular cleaning, replacement of bedding, and general hygienic measures?

6 How long do you expect your pet to live?

7 Are there any dogs or cats in the household that might take an unhealthy interest in such smaller pets?

8 Do you know where, apart from this book, to obtain information on the successful keeping of the animals you have in mind?

Getting ready for your pet

If you can answer all the above points satisfactorily, then the next
stage is to assemble the housing and accessories for your pet (see
page 49). Everything must be ready and in place before you bring
the new animal(s) home. When it is all prepared, small pets can be
obtained from several sources.

■ Pet stores

Nowadays there are many excellent pet shops. You should frequent
those that are obviously well run with sparkling clean, spacious cages
for the animals on sale and staff who gladly answer any questions you
may have. If you have any doubts concerning matters of health, speak
to your veterinarian before making a purchase.

■ Hobbyists and breeders

Other sources of small pets, particularly the fancy breeds, are
hobbyists and breeders. You can find the latter in clubs and societies
or in the advertisement columns of specialist magazines and
periodicals.

Good, clean
quarters are
essential for a
healthy pet.

Handling your pet

When selecting your pet you will certainly want to handle it and to do so correctly. Here is some useful advice.

■ Rabbits

Rabbits are easily frightened and must be handled with care. If badly handled, they can struggle violently and may injure their spinal cords, perhaps seriously. Severe fear and stress can induce a fatal heart attack in any small pet.

⚠ **Warning:** Never pick a rabbit up by its ears. If it is nervous or fractious, grasp the scruff with one hand and support the rump with the palm of your other hand. Tamer rabbits may not like the indignity of being "scruffed." With such an individual, put one hand under the chest, holding each foreleg separately between the thumb and two fingers, and, as above, take the weight with your other hand under the rump. When carrying a rabbit thus held, keep it close to your chest. The animal is then best placed on a solid nonslip surface, such as a table, but still restrained by your hands.

This shows the correct way to hold a nervous rabbit – gently but firmly.

■ Guinea pigs

Gently but firmly grasp the animal around its shoulders, lift it up, and then support the rump with your other hand.

■ Hamsters

They can be handled like guinea pigs or, if grumpy, can be scruffed, although you should remember that the scruff of a hamster can be rather large and slack because of the animal's extensive elastic cheek pouches.

Firm but very gentle handling is essential for guinea pigs.

■ Gerbils

Never pick a gerbil up by its tail – the skin may peel off! Support it on the palm of one hand and hold the base of the tail between finger and thumb of the other hand to keep it from leaping off, perhaps disastrously. It can also be gently scruffed and pressed down against the palm if extra restraint is required, but should never be lifted by the scruff.

> **Warning:** Gerbils may panic if they are restrained on their backs – don't do it.

■ Rats and mice

■ Rats can be grasped around their shoulders (with your thumb beneath the lower jaw if they are frightened and likely to bite). Nervous rats can be briefly lifted by the base of their tails.

> **Warning:** They should never be scruffed.

■ Mice can be lifted briefly by their tails and then gently scruffed by the other hand. Frequent, gentle, firm handling keeps your pet tame and amenable.

> **Warning:** Frightened mice and rats can bite.

Handle gerbils and hamsters carefully to avoid falls.

What to look for when selecting your pet

■ Rabbits

If you're a beginner or if it is to be a child's first rabbit, a Dutch rabbit, Himalayan, Netherland Dwarf, or (long-eared) Lop would fill the bill admirably. All of these breeds are known for their docility. Inspect your rabbit for signs of good health.

The coat should be clean, in good condition, with no bald spots or evidence of parasites.

Look at the hindquarters for signs of dirty, smeared fur, which indicates diarrhea.

The animal should be perky and fussing around, nose twitching, when outside its nest.

Warning: Be careful with a strange rabbit. It may bite, and it can be a hard, painful bite at that!

The ears must be clean and empty of crusts, cheesy matter, or unpleasant smelling secretions.

There must be no signs of matter or excessive watery discharge from the eyes or nose.

Breathing should be regular, silent, and at a rate of between 35 and 65 breaths per minute (up to 100 per minute for babies).

Always have a look at the prominent incisor teeth; they should be evenly balanced and not so overgrown that they nip the skin of the lips.

Look out for discoloration of the fur of the forepaws, which will accompany persistent rubbing of an irritated or inflamed nose.

■ Guinea pigs

Points to watch out for when buying a guinea pig are as follows:

There must be no discharge from eyes, ears, nose, or mouth.

The coat should be thick and shiny, not thin, flaky, or soiled.

The animal should appear alert. Check carefully for parasites (nit eggs may be seen around the ears).

The breathing should be regular and silent.

When handled, the animal should feel solid and well covered.

Droppings should be formed without evidence of diarrhea.

■ Hamsters

It is always best to buy only young hamsters. The animal you choose should inspect you as closely as you inspect it. This hamster is exactly the sort of persnickety pet that you require.

Look for an immature animal that is 7.5–10 cm/3–4 in long with wide open, beady eyes.

It should have an alert, inquisitive manner and not be alarmed by handling.

The fur should be smooth and unbroken.

It should be clean with no diarrhea.

Note: Make allowances, of course, for a hamster disturbed while napping during the daytime. Hamsters are grumpy and lethargic for a while if rudely awakened and are therefore perhaps best inspected late in the day.

■ Gerbils, rats, and mice

An acceptable gerbil, mouse, or rat should be very much
a busybody, always on the go and verging on the nosy.
Look for the following points:

The eyes, ears, nose,
mouth, and rear end
should be clean and clear.

The animal must be neither too
thin nor too fat. Mice that are
plump may well be one year old
or more and thus "senior
citizens."

Tails must be
intact, smooth-
skinned, or, in the
case of gerbils,
smooth-furred and
completely
unblemished.

It should not
resent gentle
handling and
should be quite
easy to catch.

There must be no
sign of lameness
when moving around.

The animal's fur
should be sleek
and shiny,
without any thin
or bald spots.

Housing your pets

There are many types of housing for small pets available in pet stores. However, some are too small or too flimsily built, so if you have any doubts consult your veterinarian or have the housing, particularly for rabbits, built to your specifications. Finding suitable ready-made accommodations can also sometimes be difficult in the case of pet rats. To help you make choices that will give your pet a high quality of life, I give you the basic requirements on the following pages.

Spacious, dry, draft-proof hutches must be positioned correctly, preferably in the shade and not facing into the sun or wind. Housing outdoors may not be possible in temperature extremes below 4.4°C/40°F or above 26.7°C/80°F.

Rabbits

Puffins on Puffin Island, off Anglesey, Wales, evict rabbits from their burrows during the nesting season, taking over and squatting in the holes until the chicks are reared! They are intent on keeping the rabbits out, but the difficulty of keeping rabbits in led to the use of rabbit islands in the old days. Queen Elizabeth I of England established several such water-surrounded collections to supply her kitchens.

The pet owner today hardly needs to go to such lengths. Hutches and runs are economical in space and cheap to set up, and many suitable cages are also available commercially. These excellent pets are truly energy saving, being essentially self-exercising (unlike dogs) and simple to house (unlike ponies). Since they are quiet, they are also excellent apartment pets.

■ Housing a rabbit outdoors

A hutch for, say, two medium-sized does (male rabbits often fight if housed together, and does and bucks are best housed separately), should be well built of strong timber at least 15 mm/^{1}/$_2$ in thick.

■ The dimensions should be no less than 150 x 60 x 60 cm/60 x 24 x 24 in, with two compartments, the living room and the bedroom or nesting box.

■ There should be a pitched roof sloping backward and with an overhang at the front covered with a tough waterproof material.

A hutch should be divided into two: the living area and the nesting box.

Temperature range

Rabbits prefer a temperature range of 10°–18°C/47–64°F, but are somewhat hardy outside these limits. However, you should beware of temperatures above 28°C/84°F; when it becomes that hot there is a strong risk of heat exhaustion with possibly fatal results. Should the temperature exceed 28°C/84°F, your rabbit should be moved to a cooler location or brought indoors if you have air conditioning or a cool garage or basement.

■ There should be a strong wire mesh front to one side of the living room, about 80 cm/32 in high.

■ The hutch should have legs to raise it from the ground.

■ Always allow enough room for the animals to grow.

■ The interior should be given a smooth finish – I prefer Formica.

■ The nesting box must be big enough to allow the rabbits to stretch out on their sides.

■ The solid floor should be protected either by coating with polyurethane to make it watertight, or provided with a shallow galvanized tray containing a 5-cm/2-in deep layer of litter (softwood shavings or sawdust fit the bill).

■ Wire mesh floors are undesirable; they reduce cleaning, of course, but are very hard on the rabbit's feet.

■ Any wood preservatives used must be nontoxic.

■ Hay or straw should be provided in the sleeping compartment, which is fitted with a draft-proof solid door. Side doors are far better than hatches in the roof or removable roofs. In the wild, predators tend to seize rabbits from above and, instinctively, domestic rabbits can be alarmed by hands approaching suddenly from on high.

■ A wooden panel with ventilation holes or a curtain of thick sacking should be attachable in front of the living room mesh for use in conditions of driving rain, excessive cold, etc.

Exercise runs must be moved frequently onto fresh grass.

■ Positioning the hutch

The best direction for positioning the hutch is toward the southeast, not facing directly into the wind or sun. Placing it in the shade and against a protective wall or fence is always a wise measure.

■ Be aware that wild and domestic animals may attempt to access your garden and attack your pet. Therefore, be sure the cage is secure and protected from predators.

■ Exercise runs

Supervised daily exercise indoors or outside is essential to help keep your pet fit and healthy. For outside use, build a portable tent-shaped run of mesh with a rigid wooden "skirting board" and wire mesh floor at least 100 x 200 cm/40 x 80 in. Moving it around frequently

Important

Cages and hutches must be cleaned out two or three times weekly as rabbits urinate abundantly.

Indoor exercise

When exercising your pet rabbit indoors, always make sure that your home has been "rabbit-proofed" so that there are no electrical wires or carpets to chew.

avoids the problem of the ground within the run becoming over-loaded with bacteria or parasites. Exercise runs must be covered at one end to afford shelter from the sun. Burrowing outside is seldom any problem. Be aware that ingesting too much grass, particularly in the spring, can lead to serious digestive upset. Never leave your pet unattended in its run as predators or vermin may try to attack.

Although some rabbits do not object to a harness and leash, not many agree to go for a walk like this handsome English rabbit.

Guinea pigs

Guinea pigs are less hardy than rabbits and demand more protection from the elements; therefore, they are best housed indoors in climates where temperatures range beyond 4.4–32°C/40–90°F. For breeding, a temperature between 15.5–18.5°C/59–66°F is recommended. If the temperature is not kept above 13°C/55°F, young guinea pigs do not thrive well. Conversely, if the temperature rises above 32°C/90°F, heat exhaustion, particularly in pregnant females, may occur and this can be fatal.

■ Housing a guinea pig
■ Hutches

In suitable climates, quarters for a guinea pig can be a hutch (as for a rabbit), which should be at least 120 x 60 x 45 cm/48 x 24 x 18 in to house two small guinea pigs. It is essential that the hutch should be well insulated, well lit, vermin-proof, and with sound, waterproof, draft-proof walls and flooring. Always avoid hutches with wire floors as they can cause broken legs and ulcers in the soles of the feet of guinea pigs.

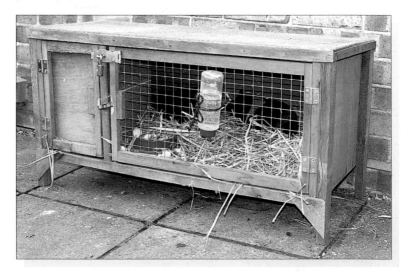

■ Cages

Suitable cages for guinea pigs are readily available in pet stores.
Dimensions should be a minimum of 65 x 35 x 35 cm/2 x 1 x 1 ft,
with a bottom tray about 12.5–15 cm/8 in deep. These cages are
easy to handle and to clean (which should be done frequently in
order to keep them odorless). A sleeping box about 25 x 15 x 15
cm/10 x 6 x 6 in with a wide entrance and flat roof (used as an
observation platform) is also appreciated.

**Guinea pigs
require a spacious
cage with plenty
of clean bedding,
such as hay or
wood shavings.**

Long-haired
guinea pigs
will require
regular
grooming.

■ Bedding

Bedding for guinea pigs may consist of wood shavings, preferably aspen, which does not contain volatile oils. However, it is best not to use straw or shavings from cedar or pine wood that may be eaten by your pets and cause stomach upsets. Some of the hay provided freely will be used by the animals as bedding. Be aware that bedding should be removed and the guinea pig quarters cleaned out at least twice a week.

Note: Guinea pigs and rabbits should never be housed together in a hutch, cage, or an outdoor run as this can be hazardous to your guinea pig.

Outdoor runs

As with rabbits, outdoor runs (permanent or portable) for guinea pigs should be set up for use in good weather. Again, outdoor exercise must be supervised to protect your pet from predators, vermin, and the elements. Never take your guinea pig out in temperatures above 29°C/85°F to avoid heatstroke, which can be fatal.

Hamsters

In the wild, hamsters live in desert areas with extremes of temperature that can range from 52°C to –3°C/128°F to 25°F within the space of 24 hours. They are hermits who prefer to live alone, accustomed to burrows where the atmosphere is one of high humidity.

■ Housing a hamster

As pets, hamsters are best kept singly for most of the time. Special hamster cages, at least 2400 cm² x 30 cm/945 in² x 10 in high, should be made of fiberglass, heavy-duty plastic (polypropylene and polycarbonate are tougher and more hamster-resistant than polyethylene, acrylene, and polystyrene), or galvanized metal but not aluminum, zinc, or wood, which are all easily chewed and can cause heavy metal toxicity.

Breeding hamsters requires careful planning; turn to page 89 for more detailed information.

■ Hamsters and other rodents love hiding away in corners so if you buy a circular cage, be sure to provide a hiding place.

■ A metal grate at the top or side is preferable to wire mesh. Hamsters should not be kept in cages where there is wire mesh with fewer than eight meshes per 5 cm/2 in, as mesh that is too big can cause facial or leg injuries.

■ Slide doors are preferable to hinged ones that easily trap tiny limbs.

■ As with rabbits, access from the side is preferable to access from above the animal.

■ Temperature range

The best temperature range for the hamster environment is 21–24°C/70–76°F. Keep pregnant and nursing females and their young at the top end of this range and males toward the bottom.

Too high a temperature is more dangerous to hamsters than one that is too low, and high temperatures and low humidity can lead to a shortened life and premature old age. In hot weather, make sure that your hamster cage is in a room where the window is open. Don't place cages by sunlit windows.

It is best to have a cage with an access door on the side wall and have the exercise wheel fixed to the cage to prevent it from falling and injuring the animal.

■ Humidity

Ideally, humidity in the hamster cage should not fall below 40 to 60 percent. To this end, make sure that water bottles are always full and put a bowl of water near the hamster cage in dry weather.

■ Exercise wheels

These are best included in the hamster cage as fixed units that are unable to topple over.

■ Bedding

This must be provided in the form of softwood aspen shavings, or shredded paper. Avoid cedar or pine shavings if possible, or air them out well as the volatile oils are irritating to the hamster's respiratory tract. Obtain clean bedding that is uncontaminated by wild rodent droppings or urine. Hamsters like absorbent cotton as a nest-making material. You should clean out soiled bedding every two or three days. Providing a small glass jar that is laid on its side in the cage often stimulates the hamster to use it as a lavatory. Empty the jar and wash it out daily

Exercise wheels and hiding places will keep your hamster amused.

Gerbils, mice, and rats

Gerbils, rats, and mice are easy and inexpensive to house, and cages of wood, aluminum, galvanized iron, or heavy plastic, or aquarium tanks of glass may be used. Wood has the disadvantage of absorbing liquid and is therefore less hygienic. It is also highly chewable! Cages do allow more opportunities to climb and smell their owners as well as see them, but can be drafty. Glass tanks are cozy, draft-free, and easier to clean but require more frequent cleaning, and are really only suitable for gerbils who produce little urine and, therefore, ammonia. In the others, ammonia buildup irritates the respiratory tissues leading to diseases like Mycoplasma pulmonis pneumonia in rats. As each species has its own special requirements, I shall deal with their housing needs separately, but for all, square or rectangular cages or tanks are preferable to circular ones. Rodents adore corners!

Gerbils
■   A heavy plastic or steel and wire cage or an aquarium tank with

This cage is ideal for gerbils who like climbing.

an area of at least 1500 cm² x 30 cm/591 in² x 12 in high with a close-fitting wire mesh cover are ideal.

■ The floor covering should be of aspen softwood shavings, with hay, or shredded paper (not newsprint) for bedding.

■ Artificial fiber bedding should not be used—the strands can get wrapped around tiny limbs, sometimes causing serious interference with blood circulation. Sand, also, is not recommended. Gerbils will burrow in it and may easily injure their faces.

■ The room temperature for gerbils should be 15–20°C/59–68°F with a maximum of 50 percent humidity.

Mice

■ Metal cages or glass tanks are best for mice—minimum dimensions are 1200 cm² x 30 cm/472 in² x 12 in high. Each mouse must have at least 260 cm²/102 in² of floor space.

■ The cage bottom should be solid and the cover tight-fitting.

■ A sleeping compartment may be provided but is not essential if there is plenty of bedding.

Rats love company—don't keep one alone.

■ The floor covering should be softwood, sawdust, wood shavings or chips, with shredded paper (not newsprint) or cotton batting as bedding. Plenty of nesting material cuts down the risk of fighting when strangers (particularly males) are introduced.

■ Ideally, the temperature should be between 15–27°C/59–81°F. Anything above 30°C/88°F can result in fatal heatstroke.

■ When planning housing for mice, bear in mind the probability of future breeding, and either be ready to provide a second cage or tank or ensure that the original one is big enough for an expanding family. Very roughly, an increase of 50 percent in floor area allows you to house double the number of animals.

Rats

■ Pet store cages for rats are frequently too small. Rats love company so it is best to keep a pair or a small group. They prefer long narrow cages with plenty of height, a selection of platforms at various levels on which to nest, and a toilet area away from food and bedding. Two rats can be housed in a cage with a floor area of 2000 cm²/787 in² and a minimum height of 30 cm/12 in.

■ The floor must be solid. Grating or mesh floors hurt rats' feet.

■ A rabbit hutch, parrot cage, or large aquarium tank can be modified to accommodate rats happily. Hutches are more fun for rats than glass tanks.

■ The housing should be lined with softwood shavings or sawdust, and shredded paper (not newsprint) should be provided for bedding.

This cage would be better if it was longer and higher.

Absorbent cotton is not desirable as strands can become entangled with rats' limbs.

■ Rats should be housed indoors in temperatures ideally between 15–27°C/59–82°F. As with the other small rodents, too high a temperature (above 30°C/88°F) can induce heatstroke.

■ Your pets should be given a piece or log of nontoxic deciduous wood such as maple or apple on which to exercise their front teeth.

Furnishing your pet's house

■ Food and water utensils

It is important that you buy the right kind of food and water containers for your pets. Food dishes must be gnaw-resistant and heavy enough to not be easily knocked over. Avoid plastic ones – apart from the tendency of both rabbits and rodents to chew them,

Water bottles like this are better than bowls.

Drinking bowls

■ Shallow bowls and dishes, of whatever material, are not good as water containers. They quickly become contaminated with bedding, droppings, and food.

some individuals are allergic to the coloring pigments in the plastic. Glazed earthenware and stainless steel dishes or bowls are best.

■ In a rabbit hutch, food hay should be placed in a hayrack attached to one of the solid walls in the living room. This avoids trampling and soiling of the hay.

■ Use the gravity-feed demand-type water bottle with a ball valve in its metal spout which clips on to the cage side or the roof grate. Various designs are available at pet stores. When installing the water bottle, make sure that any baby animals can reach the spout and that they are strong enough to activate the valve.

■ Food and water utensils of rabbits and rodents must be cleaned two or three times a week.

■ Leisure and comfort

Small rodents love the privacy of a nesting box within their house. You can buy these from pet stores in a wide range of designs but the animals will be just as happy with a washed and dried empty milk carton or similar container. Cardboard tubes (from toilet paper rolls) are great for mice and gerbils.

■ Exercise and fun accessories

■ Rabbits need exercise and providing a run or periods of freedom in a garden is very important. Remember that exercise must be supervised indoors and outside to protect your rabbit from harm.

A wide variety of accessories can be found in pet stores.

■ Gnawing logs or blocks for all rabbits and rodents are beneficial, provided that the wood is nontoxic.

■ Small rodent pets, particularly rats, like to climb. Shelves, ramps, ladders, and climbing devices in their cages give them abundant interest, exercise, and entertainment. If they are made of wood, thorough and regular cleaning of these accessories is essential. Metal is always to be preferred to wood.

■ This also applies to treadmill wheels, which should be made of

Devices such as these entertain your pets and provide hiding places.

Cardboard tubes are just as effective and as much fun as more expensive accessories and toys.

metal. Plastic ones don't last as long as metal types. For stability it is always best to have the wheels attached securely to some part of the housing. By the way, treadmills are not cruel. On the contrary, the animals really love them and they can go on and off them whenever they wish.

■ Hamsters are especially fond of wheels as are young rats and mice. Don't, however, supply your gerbils with a wheel. They sometimes damage their tails on them. What is OK for gerbils is a dish or a small sandbox filled with Fuller's earth or some washed fine sand. This can be bought from a pet store or a hardware store, but should not be dug up outdoors. Gerbils can give themselves dust baths in these.

■ You will find all sorts of toys, such as bells, mirrors, balls, etc., for gerbils at a pet store, and the ones that are made for parakeets please gerbils equally.

CHAPTER FOUR

Food for the small pet

Rabbits

Wild rabbits will eat almost anything, as the horticulturalist and arable farmer know only too well. They munch the poisonous foxglove and deadly nightshade (dangerous for pet rabbits) without any ill effects, but tend to leave the less poisonous ragwort alone. They don't like azalea, rhododendron, honeysuckle, hawthorn, dogwood, sorrel, comfrey (enjoyed by many a pet rabbit), burdock,

Daily requirements

■ A medium-sized rabbit will need about 170 g/6 oz of pellets daily.

■ Pregnant does are fed as above but the amounts must be increased gradually to twice the normal feed by the end of pregnancy.

■ Lactating does need more again. Increase the amount to three times the normal feed by the end of lactation (six to eight weeks after giving birth).

cowslip, or primrose and will usually eat nettles only under the pressure of food shortages.

Curiously, rabbits seem to detest the cuckoo pint, or arum, and yet this plant is also called *pain de lièvre*, or hare's bread, supposedly a staple ingredient of the hare's diet.

■ Pet rabbit food

Like their wild counterparts, domestic rabbits are single-stomached, hindgut fermenting herbivores. They prefer high-protein, high-carbohydrate, low-fiber portions of plants. They are fussy eaters and may reject otherwise acceptable foods because of their odor, form or texture.

The most common feeding regime for pet rabbits is to use a "complete," specially compounded rabbit food which is available commercially, and usually in the form of pellets. Although the average medium-size rabbit will eat about 170 g/6 oz of pellets daily, it has been found that feeding less pellets, 60–90 g/2–3 oz, and feeding timothy hay free-choice (as much as the rabbit wants), is often better in preventing common rabbit health problems such as obesity, digestive upsets, and hair chewing. If using this regime, it is

Note: Always include vitamin and mineral supplements in your rabbit's diet as described on page 73.

important to feed timothy hay, not alfalfa hay, as alfalfa hay is too high in calcium to be fed in large quantities in rabbits and may promote problems with crystal formation in the urinary tract.

Rabbits have a very sensitive digestive tract microflora (bacterial population) that is easily upset by sudden indiscriminate feeding, such as offering oats, cookies, rabbit treat mixes, or too many fresh greens. Although fresh greens can and should be fed, they should only be offered in small quantities, no more than 10–20 g/less than an ounce a day in the morning so that the rabbit can digest them properly.

Good choices include Brussels sprouts, broccoli, carrots, carrot tops, parsley, cabbage, beet greens, celery, chicory, kale, parsnips, snow peas, and spinach. Wild plants, such as dandelion leaves, clover, coltsfoot, comfrey, cow parsnip, knapweed, shepherd's purse, and chickweed can also be offered, but avoid areas where pesticides may have been sprayed and wash food thoroughly before offering.

Young rabbits under six months of age are particularly sensitive to digestive upset, and it is best not to offer any fresh greens until after they are six months old. Even then, introduce greens slowly over one to two weeks to allow time for a gradual change in the microbial flora.

Never give wilted greens or kitchen or table waste. Most lettuce (other than Romaine) has little nutritive value and should not be offered in favor of the other greens mentioned. Spoiled greens can make your rabbit ill. Don't allow uneaten greens to lie in the cage where they will ferment and rot or get moldy. Remove leftovers promptly.

It is important to establish a routine feeding schedule; do not vary the times of feedings and do not make sudden changes in the quantity or types of foods fed. Never feed your rabbit any of the poisonous plants listed on page 72; make sure the food is at room temperature; never give food directly from the refrigerator.

■ Water

Although wild rabbits and their domesticated cousins may seldom drink if feeding on succulent plant material with a high water content, clean, fresh water must always be at hand for pet rabbits – winter and summer. It is a myth that rabbits don't need water. Unlike humans, who perspire when the weather is too hot, rabbits regulate their body temperature through increased breathing and greater intake of fluids. For this reason, rabbits drink more water than usual on hot days.

Rabbits that are fed almost exclusively on dry commercial food and nursing does need to have an abundant supply of water available at all times. Indeed, every pet rabbit should have free access to as much fresh clean water as it wants. Refill the water bottle every day

■ Daily requirements

A rabbit eats approximately four percent of its body weight in food each day, so an adult rabbit of, say, 4.5 kg/10 lb in weight would need around 75 g/2^1/$_2$ oz of such a concentrate mixture daily, plus about 100 g/3^1/$_2$ oz of good hay. The best hay to feed is young hay. High quality young hay is fresh-smelling and slightly greenish in color. Old hay has not only lost much of its nutritive value, it is dusty. Hay dust can be quite irritable to a rabbit's sensitive nasal passages. Although hay is best provided free choice, it is unwise to give unlimited quantities of concentrates. Rabbits easily put on a lot of excess fat and it can drastically shorten their lives.

Poisonous plants

Wild plants that you must never feed to domestic rabbits include: anemone, wild arum, autumn crocus, bindweed, bluebells, bryony, buttercup, celandine, dog mercury, elder, figwort, fool's parsley, foxglove, hemlock, henbane, nightshades, poppy, toadflax, and traveler's-joy, or wild clematis.

with fresh water at room temperature and clean the water bottle thoroughly daily to prevent bacterial buildup.

■ Diet and tooth disease

Recently, some experts have suggested that because of the high incidence of tooth disease in pet rabbits, which can have extremely serious consequences, it would be best to omit concentrates from the diet altogether and feed the animals in a way more closely resembling that of their wild relatives where the teeth and jaws are constantly well exercised. They recommend nothing but free choice hay and good fresh greens. However, it is known that tooth problems also have a genetic origin, so it is better to avoid the problem altogether and not buy a rabbit with bad teeth or consult your veterinarian on how best to manage bad teeth.

■ Freshness

If you have only one or two rabbits, don't buy large quantities of food. It is better to buy small quantities of fresh materials frequently. Stored pellets and other forms of concentrates lose valuable vitamins, essential oils, etc. When purchasing pellets, choose those that are the greenest and have the freshest smell, or look for a milling or expiration date.

■ Vitamins and minerals

A block of mineral lick should always be hung in the rabbit's quarters. Instinctively your pet will lick and nibble this to obtain any extra minerals it needs. It is also a wise precaution to supplement the water supply with vitamin drops. Suitable preparations are available at the pet store – follow the dosage directions on the label.

A mineral lick block will enable your rabbit to take instinctively as many minerals as it requires.

Summary for feeding rabbits

The basic rules for feeding rabbits are:
■ Weigh concentrates and timothy hay
■ Supply small and varied quantities of greens and roots in the morning
■ Never neglect water supply
■ Make sure your pet gets lots of exercise; obesity in rabbits can lead to heart disease and other ailments

Guinea pigs

Guinea pigs are, of course, vegetarians and resemble other rodents in many respects but they do have some special requirements. Take, for example, vitamin C. Most other animals make this vitamin in their bodies, but the guinea pig – along with humans, the great apes, the fruit bat, and (as if you haven't guessed) the red-vented bulbul bird – must get adequate vitamin C from its food to avoid coming down with scurvy. Other essential elements in the guinea pig's diet are vitamins E and K, and fiber, which is present in hay. Hay must be given to stop animals from eating their bedding or "barbering" (chewing each other's hair).

■ The correct diet

A correct diet for guinea pigs is composed of concentrates (in mash or pellet form), which are obtainable from pet stores, together with green food, hay, and water. In green food I include fruit and certain root crops.

■ Change the different ingredients on successive days to give as much variety as possible.

■ Wash all greens and thaw out any frozen roots before feeding.

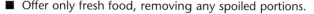
■ Offer only fresh food, removing any spoiled portions.

■ Make sure the hay is free of thistles, which can damage those delicate little mouths.

■ Daily feeding requirements

If you give about a tablespoon of some of the items in each of the following groups to your guinea pig every day, you can be sure that all the ingredients essential for a healthy life are included:

1 Fresh guinea pig-specific pellets from the pet store. (Check the milling date; vitamin C deteriorates over time. Never feed pellets that are over three months old.)

2 Hay: this should always be fed free-choice.

3 Fruit: apples, oranges, grapes, peaches, and pears, and others high in vitamin C.

4 Dandelion, groundsel, shepherd's purse, cow parsley, sow thistle, cover, chickweed, plantains, vetches, varieties of grass.

5 Carrot, turnip, cabbage, lettuce, kale, marigolds, bramble cuttings, prunings from elm and ash.

■ Water

Adequate, clean, fresh water must always be available. Even when your pet is taking in lots of green foods, you cannot rely on it getting all the water it needs that way. Too dry a diet can lead to dehydration. Although commercial guinea pig pellets are supplemented with vitamin C, it is best to dissolve a 250 mg tablet of vitamin C into the animal's water every time you change it, which should be at least three times a week.

> **Note:** Once a week it is a good idea to give a pinch of bone meal (sterilized) and a pinch of dried yeast. In the winter, a drop of cod liver oil should be mixed with the food every two or three days.

Hamsters

Hamsters are easy to feed and there are several ways of going about it.
Variety is essential, and you can try feeding grains, carrots, clover (but
not grass), dandelions, salad, bread, fruit, and dog biscuits (good for
the teeth). Pelleted or other forms of ready-prepared food for rodents,
mice, and laboratory animals can be obtained from pet stores and
provide an excellent balanced core to the diet.

■ Feeding guidelines

■ Hamsters can be given free quantities of food but do be sure to
clean out uneaten portions daily, otherwise your pets will hoard them
and they will decay.
■ Do not store foods for long periods (they lose their vitamin
content) and make sure they do not become contaminated with wild
rodent droppings.
■ Wash all fruit and green food before feeding.
■ It is normal for hamsters to eat their own droppings. The latter
contain vitamins B and K that are produced in the bowels.

■ Water

A supply of fresh clean water must always be available. Never let a
water bottle run dry. Lack of water for 24 hours can cause a weight
loss of 10 g/^{1}/3 oz or more; in youngsters, particularly in warm
weather, it may have fatal results.

Note: Some hamsters adore pieces of bread and butter. Take it
easy! Too much fat can cause obesity, heart trouble, and other
health problems. Avoid feeding too many sunflower seeds.

Gerbils

Some desert-dwelling species of gerbil survive on wind-blown seeds and little else. Most gerbils prefer to take food back to their burrows to eat and those that inhabit the colder regions are hamster-like in their hoarding. Mongolian gerbils have been known to store as much as 20 kg/44 lb of seeds.

■ A balanced diet

As pets, gerbils need a basic balanced diet with a fairly high protein content supplemented with a variety of other items.

Store-bought gerbil mix

Typically, gerbil/hamster mixes contain seeds, grains, nuts, dried vegetables, and some dried egg. If you want to make a supplementary gerbil mix, take equal parts of the following:
- Seeds (sunflower, linseed, etc.)
- Oats, wheat, flaked maize, wheat germ, millet, sugarless cereals
- Peanuts

Store the mixture in a well-sealed tin in a cool, dry place. These diets can be offered as a treat in small amounts, 5 ml/1 tsp per day, but should not form the sole diet for your pet as they are too high in fat and too low in calcium.

Premixed diets, which are suitable for both hamsters and gerbils, are available at pet stores as are balanced pellet foods for rabbits, mice, and rats, which are also suitable. Check on the package label to see that the protein content is at least 20 percent and that the food is not past its sell-by date.

■ Vegetables and fruit

Other foods that can be given occasionally include the following: vegetables, washed and dried greens and roots, washed and dried wild plants, such as dandelion, chickweed, and clover, and fruit of all kinds. Remember that only thorough washing removes all traces of pesticides, so wash all fresh fruit, vegetables, and plants before feeding them to your pet.

⚠ Caution

Sunflower seeds are very rich in fat and low in calcium. Gerbils adore them, but if they eat too many, obesity and skeletal disease can result. Too much in the way of green vegetables, particularly items like lettuce with a high water content, can cause digestive upsets and diarrhea. I repeat that you should give these foods only occasionally and then in small amounts (about one teaspoon only).

Owners like to treat their gerbil pets to snacks, such as chocolates, potato chips, popcorn, etc. Plain popcorn is alright, but chocolate can be toxic and most salty snacks are dangerously high in salt and should be avoided.

Rats and mice

Wild species eat a whole range of foods. Brown rats can thrive almost anywhere and will eat anything from putrid waste and young birds, to rabbit droppings and lubricating grease! More salubriously, the muskrat dines on freshwater mussels and crayfish. A species such as the jumping mouse lives on fruit, seeds, and insects and this is typical of the main diet of the majority of the group.

Surprisingly, cheese isn't the thing for your tame mouse or rat. It isn't even one of their favorite foods and too much of it may produce strong-smelling urine.

■ Proprietary foods

Specially balanced proprietary mouse and rat foods can be bought from the pet store.

■ Best breeding results are obtained with diets containing 25 to 40 percent protein.

■ Proprietary foods should be supplemented with a little green food and fruit three times a week.

■ They should not be stored for long, and should be protected from contamination by vermin.

■ Where cereals or food pellets are stored for any length of time, watch that they don't get infested with grain bugs. Store food in tightly sealed containers.

■ Homemade mixes

■ **For mice** If you want to make up your own diets, a good one for mice is four parts oats, one part canary seed, and one part white millet. In addition, give a little dandelion, chickweed, apple, or raw

dark green vegetable on alternate days. Remember to clean out old food every day.

■ **For rats** You can use a variable mixture of some of the following: dog biscuit, bran, oats, beans, cabbage, carrots, bread, fruit, bits of cooked meat or fish, hard-cooked egg. Meat and fish are best given only once or twice weekly. A drop of cod-liver oil and a tiny pinch of dried yeast once a week are also valuable supplements. Both mice and rats can be fed free-choice, but again, you must clean out all remains of food every day.

Water

For rats and mice, fresh, clean water must be available at all times, even though they may drink little.

CHAPTER FIVE

Breeding

Rabbits

You'll find that it's no joke about the rabbit's enthusiasm for multiplication; suffice it to say that after being introduced into Australia, rabbits took a mere 50 years to colonize that vast island.

Rabbits don't have an estrus – heat cycle – (unlike rodents) and can breed at any time of year. Ovulation, the shedding of fertile eggs from the ovary, does not occur spontaneously as in women or in animals such as the dog or cow, but is triggered by the act of mating. Non-breeding females should be spayed, as uterine cancer is very common in rabbits. Neutered males will have less odor and be less likely to spray urine to mark their territory.

■ Litters

Rabbits can have several litters of two to eight young each year. The average litter size is five but it can be as large as ten. The most prolific breed of rabbit is the Norfolk Star, which can produce 90 to 100 young per year. The general rule, though, should be to not exceed three litters per year for the sake of the health and long life of your pet doe.

■ Mating

If there is no estrus cycle in rabbits, how do you know when to put the buck and the doe together? Estrus, the time when ripe eggs are present in the ovary, can sometimes be detected by observing the vulva, which may enlarge and become purplish at this time. However, this sign isn't always present and, even if it is, some does won't accept the buck. The test is to see how the doe reacts when introduced to the buck – always take the doe to the buck, never the reverse; otherwise, the female may attack the male, possibly injuring him. If you have more than one buck, try the doe with each of them.

Nest building

The babies are usually prepared for by the doe who makes a nest lined with soft fur plucked from her own coat. It is best to provide a shallow nesting box, 5–7 cm/2–3 in deep, in the sleeping compartment of the hutch. The box is lined with sawdust and hay or straw chopped into lengths of 10–15 cm/ 4–6 in. If the doe does not contribute much fur to the nest on the day before she gives birth, add some tufts of fur saved from previous pregnancies, if possible.

Sometimes the doe shows her fickle nature by turning down one suitor only to fling herself passionately at the next.

■ Pregnancy

Pregnancy lasts around one month (28 to 34 days) in rabbits but approximately 47 days in hares. Does may accept the buck at any time during pregnancy or false pregnancy.

■ **False pregnancy** (pseudopregnancy) is a common phenomenon in rabbits and can last about two-and-a-half weeks. The milk glands swell and the doe may actually begin to prepare a nest for her phantom young.

False pregnancy can be due to an infertile mating, although it frequently follows a successful mating where the embryos die and are reabsorbed into the mother's body some time during the pregnancy period. It is believed that more than half the litters actually conceived are reabsorbed in this way. This curious "change of mind" by the doe's body is perfectly normal in most cases and seems to be Nature's last-minute attempt at population control. An expert can detect pregnancy by gently feeling the doe's abdomen as early as nine days after mating.

■ Birth

The young are generally born at night. The event is rarely observed by the owner, the whole process taking 10 to 30 minutes with seldom any complications demanding veterinary assistance. Very occasionally there is a gap of several hours or even a day between the birth of one part of the litter and another. Each baby is born with its placenta (afterbirth) which the doe eats – a sensible provision by Nature that prevents fouling of the nest. After being licked clean by their mother, the babies (sometimes called kittens) promptly seek out the maternal teats and start nursing. If necessary, kittens can be fostered onto another doe if the latter's young are the same age and the switch is begun before they are three weeks old.

■ In normal births to does having a first litter, about one percent of babies are stillborn. Overall, the ratio of male to female babies is exactly 50:50.

■ If a doe is mated while nursing a small litter she can become

These very young kittens are wild European rabbits.

True or false?

Up to the middle of the eighteenth century there were occasional reports, sometimes emanating from learned medical sources, of women giving birth to rabbits. In 1726, Mary Toft of Godalming in Surrey, England, achieved considerable notoriety by her extensively circulated statements that she bore rabbits. Mr. St. André, surgeon and anatomist to the Royal Household, published a pamphlet supporting her story with engravings of the rabbits "taken from life." Other eminent doctors also backed her up. Eventually, after being closely watched, the curious Ms. Toft was exposed and confessed to being a fraud, but for a short time thereafter rabbit was excluded from most English dining tables.

pregnant, whereas if she is nursing a larger litter (the minimum size varies with breed), the pregnancy will be curtailed after about five days.

■ Gradually increase the food of a pregnant doe so that at the time of birth she should be getting three times the normal ration. It is a good idea to put a shelf into a breeding hutch so that the mother can get some respite from time to time from the incessant demands of her brood.

■ Development of the kittens

At birth young rabbits are helpless, with their eyes and ears closed and only a light down instead of fur. By the end of the first week of life the fur begins to grow; after ten days the eyes open; after twelve days the ears open; and by sixteen to eighteen days the kittens have begun to leave the nest and to nibble solid food.

■ **Note:** Do not touch the kittens before they begin to emerge from the nest. If you do, the doe may kill them. Does may also kill their

young if they have too little milk and sometimes for psychological
reasons that are not understood.

■ Feeding the kittens

■ The kittens nurse for six to eight weeks and after weaning should
be kept in pairs or colonies, although young males are best housed
singly from three months of age to prevent fighting. It is extremely
difficult but possible to raise a baby rabbit on the bottle, but cow's
milk isn't rich enough for the job since it contains only four percent
protein, whereas rabbit milk contains ten percent.

■ **Making formula milk** To make a suitable formula, extra protein in
the form of 15 g/^{1}/$_2$ oz of calcium caseinate per 280 g/10 fl oz of
cow's milk must be added. This mixture is suitable until the kittens are
seven days old after which the calcium caseinate must be increased to
17 g/^{3}/$_5$ oz per 280 g/10 fl oz of milk. At fourteen days, the caseinate
must be raised yet again to 20 g/^{3}/$_4$ oz per 280 g/10 fl oz of milk. The
caseinate is mixed with the milk by whisking in a blender and will
keep for several days in a refrigerator. Feeding should be given every
three hours, beginning at 6 AM and finishing at midnight. The milk
mixture should be warmed to the kitten's body temperature before
feeding by pipette or from a doll's feeding bottle complete with nipple.

Reproductive life

Rabbits become sexually mature at four months (small breeds)
or six months (large breeds). Don't breed for the first time until
young does are at least six months old (small breeds) or ten
months old (large breeds). Males have an active reproductive
life of three to four years. Females should be retired from
breeding at two to three years of age. The life span of rabbits is
six or seven years on average, although the record is held by a
doe that reached eighteen years!

Guinea pigs

Female guinea pigs become sexually mature as early as four to five weeks of age. Males are fertile somewhat later at eight to ten weeks. If breeding is your aim, a good age to start mating a female is when she is 12 to 13 weeks old, while the bones of her birth canal are still flexible and are able to "give" easily during birth.

■ Mating

The female guinea pig, usually called appropriately the "sow," can be allowed to mix freely with the male or "boar" while she is not pregnant. You can keep one sow and one boar or as many as 12 sows and one boar in a breeding group. Unlike hamsters, there are no special mating instructions for the peaceable guinea pig.

A nesting box with around 0.25 m²/2.6 sq ft of floor area, lined with soft hay or shredded paper (not newsprint), can be laid down for a pregnant sow, but is not essential provided you make sure there is plenty of bedding hay available in which she can form a nest for herself.

These sociable creatures get along well in groups and even after the birth it is perfectly correct, if there is adequate space, to leave a bunch of moms and their broods together for communal rearing. It is best, however, to remove the boar, or boars, from the sows if you suspect that the latter are pregnant or at least as soon as the young are born. Some owners leave a boar and several sows permanently

together and such gradually enlarging colonies are rarely the scene of disharmony or squabbling, but the steady population expansion will certainly lead to epidemics of disease if enough living space is not provided. In these communal systems each sow needs a minimum of approximately 1300 cm^2/200 in^2 of floor space. Some experts consider that the optimum colony size is one boar to twelve sows.

■ Courtship displays

During mating, you may witness the courtship display typical of guinea pigs (and also of certain other rodents such as chinchillas, agoutis, coipus, and porcupines). The male wags his rear end, quivers his body, and makes sprightly hops. He also sprays urine on his mate.

■ Estrus

The female has an estrus cycle of five to six days and is "in heat" for only a few hours. Once mated, the female rapidly becomes non-receptive to the male. Estrus commonly occurs soon after the birth of a litter and there is no harm in mating a female again at this time.

Pregnancy

In the guinea pig, this lasts from 59 to 72 days with an average of 63 days. Litter size is between one and 13 with an average of four. Two or three litters are born each year under suitable conditions and the mother nurses her young for two to three months. Wild cavies produce young only once a year with only one or two babies to a litter but these little fellows begin feeding themselves at one day old.

Hamsters

Female hamsters normally become mature at the early age of six to eight weeks, although successful mating has been recorded in animals only four weeks old. If you want to breed hamsters, use young females, preferably ones under eight months of age. A good time is when they are about two months old. The duration of pregnancy is the shortest for any mammal that produces fully developed babies – 15 to 18 days. Several litters can be produced in a year, each averaging four to twelve young.

■ Mating

The estrus (heat) cycle lasts about four days. To test whether a female is in heat, place her in a container, such as a large can lined with paper, or even a bucket, and introduce a male. If she is in heat she will flatten her spine and then arch it downward and accept the male. Keep an eye on things in case fighting breaks out. If the couple get along well, leave them together for 15 minutes to one hour, but

Baby hamsters nurse from their mother for a period of three to four weeks before taking solids.

still remain alert for trouble. If there
is no sign of spine-flattening within
ten minutes of the introduction,
return the female to her cage
and repeat the procedure on
the following day.

■ **False pregnancy**
(pseudopregnancy) sometimes
occurs and lasts for eight to ten days.

■ Pregnancy

The female hamster's cage should be placed in a quiet place when she
is pregnant. Darken the part of the cage over the nest by covering it
with a suitable piece of metal or plastic. Shredded paper, in strips not
more than about 0.5 cm/^{1}/$_4$ in wide, is the best material for bedding in
a breeding cage. It is clean and won't entangle the newborn babies.

■ Birth

This is usually a trouble-free process that occurs at night. The mother
will nurse her young for three to four weeks. Make sure that she has
all the food she wants during the pregnancy and lactation period.

Gerbils

In the wild, gerbils organize themselves into large social groups comprising between one and three adult males, two to seven adult females, and several subadults and juveniles. They all live together in a jealously guarded burrow, chasing off strange gerbils should any come a-calling – with one exception, which prevents the gerbils from becoming dangerously inbred. Female gerbils leave their group when they come into estrus (heat), visit another burrow where they are permitted to enter, mate, and then return to their own community. The young born thereafter are brought up not by their mother and father, but by their mother and "uncles."

This female gerbil is carrying a baby into her nesting box.

■ Mating

Pet gerbils can breed at any time of the year although most sexual activity is in the summer. If you decide to mate a couple of gerbils, it is best to do this before they are sexually mature, at nine to ten weeks old, and to use a pair from the same litter. Unrelated gerbils, particularly adults, can fight furiously – even to the death – and introducing such individuals requires much care, supervision, and patience by the owner who should at first arrange brief encounters that, little by little, can be extended as the days go by.

■ Estrus and pregnancy

Female gerbils come into estrus (heat) every four to ten days until they are 15 to 20 months old. During her breeding life one female may produce up to ten litters (one litter every 30 to 40 days) with an average litter size of five pups. If a female is mated at the first estrus after giving birth while still nursing more than two pups, the resulting pregnancy may be extended by means of the natural physiological mechanism called delayed implantation. Such a long pregnancy can last for up to 42 days. However, normally pregnancy lasts for 24 to 26 days.

■ If a nonfertile mating occurs, it is occasionally followed by a false pregnancy of 14 to 16 days.

■ Diet during pregnancy

When a female is pregnant (you may suspect this having watched the mating or heard the rhythmic drumming of the male gerbil's hind legs as he becomes sexually excited), cut down on fattening food like sunflower seeds but increase the amount of protein in the diet by adding a little dried milk powder to the food.

■ Birth

A nesting box is not essential for an expectant gerbil mom, but extra supplies of bedding in the form of soft paper should be provided for her to use in nest construction. It isn't necessary to remove the male when birth occurs. Gerbils are monogamous and the male will generally do no harm to growing pups.

■ Around 75 percent of newborn pups survive – weak ones are born dead or die during the first few days after birth. Don't be too upset – it is natural, and almost all of the pups that perish are congenitally defective in some way.

■ Sometimes, mothers will kill and eat their litters or desert them.

This can be caused by the stress of excessive disturbance, overcrowding, or the presence of disease in the mother's breast tissue. Less frequently, males exhibit cannibalism (jealousy perhaps?) but usually they make good fathers.

■ Baby gerbils are born hairless, deaf, blind, and toothless but grow amazingly quickly and for that reason the mother's food should be increased immediately after giving birth. Hair starts to grow at six days old and eyes open at ten to twelve days.

■ The pups begin eating solids at between 16 and 20 days and are weaned at 21 to 24 days.

■ After weaning, the youngsters can remain in the parental cage, but they should be sexed at eight weeks and males and females then placed in separate new accommodations – otherwise, inbreeding is likely to begin.

Two-week-old gerbil babies will soon be ready to begin eating solids.

Mice and rats

■ Mice

Male and female mice can be left together permanently during
their breeding life. The heat cycle in the female mouse occurs about
every five days. Mice become sexually mature at six to eight weeks.
Pregnancy lasts 20 or 21 days but can be as long as 28 days where
mating occurs at the first heat period after giving birth. Litter size is
up to 20 with an average of seven. (A record 32 young born to a
house mouse in 1961 is the largest litter produced by any wild
mammal at a single birth.)

■ Rats

Female rats should be put into separate cages at least one week
before giving birth. Rats become sexually mature at between
40 and 60 days. The heat cycle lasts four to five days. Pregnancy in

**It is very important that baby rodents should not be handled
during the first two weeks of life.**

Caution

Rats and mice nurse their young for around three weeks.
Never handle the young or change the bedding for at least
one week after birth, and it is best left until they are two
weeks old. At around two weeks of age, mice reach the so-
called "flea age" and, when disturbed, may leap straight up
into the air in alarm.

rats lasts from 21 to 23 days. The litter size is up to 16 with an
average of 11 young.

■ Scent and fertility

Odors that contain sex hormones (pheromones) are very important
in the sex life of mice. The more female mice that are kept in one
enclosure, the more infertile they become; the "sex smell" of one
another reduces their fertility. Male odors work in the opposite way,

but only if the scent comes from the female mouse's own mate. Infidelity, in the form of the introduction of a strange male, not only continues to block the female's fertility, but also actually kills any developing embryos within her womb.

Hand-rearing pet babies

■ Hand-rearing is seldom called for but the necessity could arise if unweaned youngsters were suddenly orphaned for some reason or the mother developed mastitis or agalactia (absence of milk). Of course, in certain circumstances such babies might be fostered by another lactating female with young of approximately the same age.

■ If the mother will not accept the strange baby or babies, you can try smearing a touch of menthol vapor rub on both the nose of the foster mother and the bodies of the babies. The menthol masks the foreign scent of the new arrivals.

■ It is often necessary to resort to artificial milk feeding. The kind of milk powder available at pet stores for rearing cats will normally be satisfactory. Make it up with water as for kittens, following the instructions on the package, and administer with an eyedropper or hypodermic (insulin) syringe obtainable at a pharmacy – without the needle, naturally.

■ Feed a little and often, enough to make the stomach plump, and judge your progress by weighing the babies if you have a small enough scale.

■ Start weaning at the appropriate time (see above) by introducing wholegrain bread soaked in milk or thin oat cereal.

■ Keep the babies warm, preferably by hanging an infrared bulb (of the type used in bathrooms and by farmers) over them at a distance of no less than 1 m/3 ft.

CHAPTER SIX

General care of your pet

■ Hygiene

This is vital in ensuring a long and healthy life for your pet and in controling unwanted odors.

■ Hutch or cage floor litter should be changed twice a week (daily for does with young).

■ Bedding should be replaced once a week except where unweaned babies are in a nest.

■ The animal's quarters should be carefully cleaned at these times and a mild animal disinfectant spray should be applied and then dried off. Never use phenol/carbolic acid-type disinfectants. Buy approved pet disinfectants from the pet store or use so-called ampholytic disinfectants or the kind used in catering for disinfecting glassware.

■ In summer, rabbit and guinea pig hutches should be scrubbed thoroughly with hot water and mild disinfectant, rinsed, and then allowed to dry while the occupiers are outside.

Distress in rodents

Do watch out for signs of sudden distress in small rodent pets. Certain noises, including very high-pitched ones that cannot be picked up by human ears, can affect these creatures. The source could even be a computer, telephone, or television remote control device. If such things are seen to upset your pets, relocate their housing well away from the noisemaker.

Grooming

Rabbits Although they generally groom themselves, there is no harm in grooming your rabbit if it gives you both pleasure. Also, it makes the animal tamer and easier to handle as well as assisting the molting process at the end of the winter. Plucking the loose fur will help prevent hairballs, a potentially serious condition in rabbits. The luxurious, long-haired Angora must be groomed daily with a soft brush, applying it in the direction of the natural lie of the coat to help prevent matting of the fur.
Guinea pigs Not essential for most guinea pigs, but some long-haired ones can be groomed using a small, very soft brush.

■ Food and water containers must be cleaned daily, preferably put through a hot wash cycle in a dishwasher or scalded with boiling water.

■ Playtime and grooming

Handle and play with your small pet at least four or five times a week. Feed it tidbits from your fingers and groom it gently with a soft brush. Grooming is desirable but not essential for most of these animals. It is, however, very important for longer-haired breeds like the Angora rabbit and Peruvian guinea pig, and for any individual whose coat becomes soiled or stained somehow. The grooming equipment made for cats is ideal for rabbits and guinea pigs. Stains and sticky patches can be removed with moist cloths or a mild pet shampoo, being sure to rinse the area thoroughly after use to remove any residue.

■ Sexing

It goes without saying that the major requirement, if you decide to breed your small pets, is to know what sex they are; not always easy if they are young. Here is how to go about it.

Rabbits

Male rabbits have a round genital opening. Gentle pressure around it will extrude the penis. Female rabbits have a slit-like genital opening.

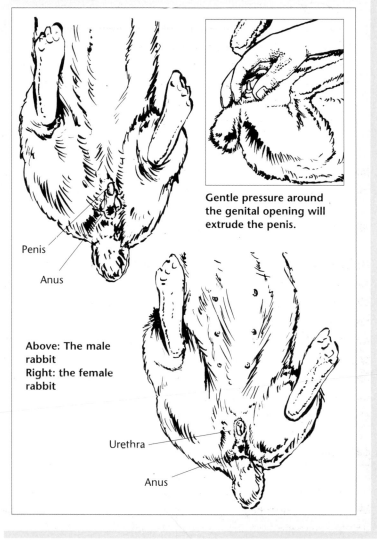

Gentle pressure around the genital opening will extrude the penis.

Penis

Anus

Above: The male rabbit
Right: the female rabbit

Urethra

Anus

Guinea pigs

The genitalia of male and female guinea pigs are very similar at first sight. However, by pressing gently on each side of the genital opening the penis can be extruded in the male.

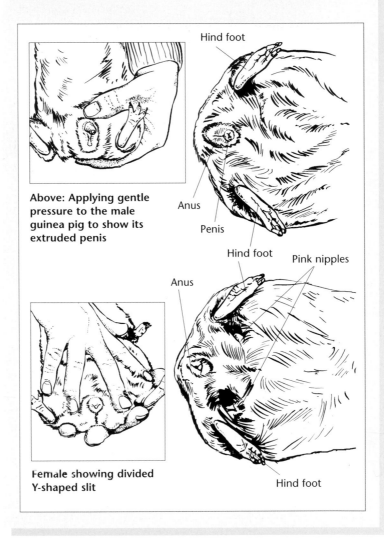

Hind foot

Above: Applying gentle pressure to the male guinea pig to show its extruded penis

Anus

Penis

Hind foot

Pink nipples

Anus

Female showing divided Y-shaped slit

Hind foot

Hamsters

Even when young, female hamsters are easy to recognize by the lines of teats on their abdomens. When the fur grows you may have to hunt carefully for them. Also, the male has an elongated hind end and there is a prominent bulge just before the tail. The female's hind end is more rounded and has no bulge.

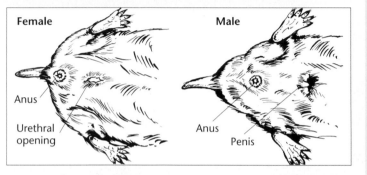

Female   Male

Anus

Urethral opening

Anus

Penis

Gerbils

To examine a gerbil's genitalia, don't turn it onto its back, but rather (and this is the one occasion when you can do it), raise the animal off the ground by briefly picking it up by the base of its tail. Males have a darkish oblong-shaped scrotum beneath the tail, whereas females have a small vagina close to the anus.

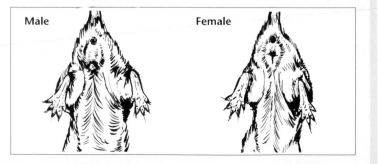

Male   Female

Rats

The distance between the anus and the tiny genital opening is distinctly greater in males than in females (at three weeks of age, for example, 1.25 cm/0.5 in as opposed to just under 1 cm/0.39 in). Also, you should be able to see the slight swelling, even in young males, where the scrotum will be.

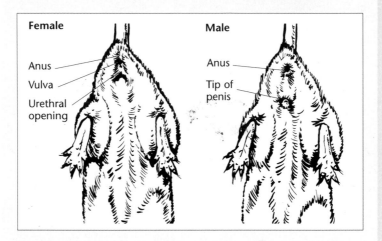

Mice

In mice, as in rats, the distance between the anus and the genital opening is greater (almost twice as far) in males as compared to females. Gentle pressure around the opening will cause the penis to protrude in males.

Sexing is more difficult in very young mice. At two to three weeks of age, females have ten nipples that are clearly visible on their still hairless bellies. At three to four weeks old, gently pulling the skin of the male's rear underbelly toward the front will cause the testes to descend into the scrotum.

CHAPTER SEVEN

When small pets fall ill

Rabbits

Although generally hardy, trouble-free creatures, rabbits do sometimes fall ill and, as a species, have their peculiar problems.

■ Myxomatosis

This is undoubtedly the most notorious rabbit disease. A viral disease, it was first described in 1893 in domestic rabbits in Uruguay. Apparently, the germ is widespread among wild South American rabbits that have built up a comparatively strong resistance to its attack. Attempts to control the rabbit population in Australia were made fairly successfully by introducing the virus, although strains of

✚ The pet-owner's approach to the sick rabbit

As with other types of pets, it is essential to seek professional help from a veterinarian if you are troubled by something you do not understand. There are a large number of illnesses that can afflict the different organs and systems of the rabbit. Most have been extensively studied by scientists and treatment methods worked out. As with all medicine, diagnosis is what counts; anyone can read up on the treatment if he or she knows exactly what the matter is.

rabbits resistant to the disease soon appeared.

In 1953, the virus was deliberately introduced into France; it quickly got out of control and swept through the largely nonresistant rabbit population of Europe, causing almost 100 percent fatalities. It arrived in Britain in October 1953, striking first at colonies in Kent and Sussex. Wild rabbits are the natural reservoir host in North America. A highly virulent strain exists in California and Oregon and is spread by mosquitoes and other arthropod vectors.

It is spread by the bite of rabbit fleas in Europe and by mosquitoes in Australia, and also by direct and indirect contact. Among wild rabbits, myxomatosis spreads most rapidly in the spring during their peak breeding season. The reason for this is the intriguing fact that rabbit fleas themselves breed only on pregnant rabbits.

■ Symptoms

After an incubation period of two to eight days, the animal shows signs of a cold with swelling of the nose, ears, eyelids, and other body openings. Puffy, jellylike swellings form beneath the skin over the body. There is dullness, lack of appetite, loss of weight, and, finally, death after 11 to 18 days.

Treatment

This is very difficult, and antibiotics are of little value. Prevention can be achieved by vaccination and controling fleas or other insect carriers. Domestic rabbits are not commonly at risk but if you live in the country and have wild rabbits entering your garden, precautions to be taken would include:

■ Protect the rabbit hutch from penetration by outsiders with wire mesh – five strands per cm/10 strands per in.

■ Using insecticides and restricting the use of runs when you hear of myxomatosis in the area.

■ Best of all is a protective vaccine that is now available. Consult your veterinarian.

■ Where vaccination is not available, keeping your rabbit indoors to prevent exposure is advisable.

General symptoms

I have grouped general symptoms of poor health in the following
section with some comments on first aid, the veterinarian's approach,
and a little background.

■ Loss of weight

This can be due to various diseases, including pseudotuberculosis,
tapeworm cysts, coccidiosis, or other forms of chronic infection.
The veterinarian will take specimens of droppings to look for parasitic
coccidia or other bugs. If the diagnosis is coccidiosis, antibiotics may
be prescribed. Where other diseases are the cause, your veterinarian
may prescribe other medications. Seek advice early.

■ Fur balls

Sometimes loss of weight accompanied by lack of appetite and
perhaps diarrhea is due to fur balls in the stomach. As in long-haired
cats, excessive grooming and swallowing of hair gradually builds up
a firm, sticky mass in the stomach. Unlike cats, rabbits cannot vomit,
so the hair remains trapped in the stomach. This condition can
usually be treated medically by your veterinarian, but in some cases
surgery (gastrotomy) under general anesthesia is required.

Consult your veterinarian

Much time, suffering, and money spent on patent medicines
can be saved by loading a sick rabbit into a carrying box and
whisking it off to the veterinarian. Many rabbit conditions need
the same sort of treatment – antibiotics, injections, simple
surgery, or whatever – that is given for similar conditions in
humans, horses, dogs, or elephants.

■ Teeth problems

Wild rabbits seldom visit the dentist. It isn't because they're
frightened of the dental chair but because they exercise their teeth
cropping grass and other fiber-containing plants, and choose a
healthy diet. Pet rabbits have too easy a life. Commercial (pet store)
rabbit diets need little chewing, and many owners provide food that
is rich in starch and low in roughage. Also, vitamin/mineral
deficiencies or imbalances – bacterial infection or a poor genetic
background – may be present. The result is the formation of plaque,
caries (cavities), weakening and overgrowth of the teeth. This can
then lead to secondary, potentially serious disease.

■ **Dental problems** are common in rabbits. If you suspect anything
is wrong with your rabbit's chewing, if there are any odd lumps
around the jaws, or if the front teeth seem rather long, consult

Rabbit's skull

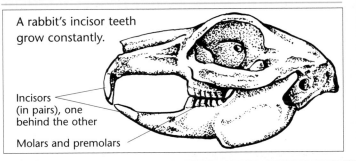

A rabbit's incisor teeth
grow constantly.

Incisors
(in pairs), one
behind the other

Molars and premolars

your veterinarian. Dental check-ups and, where necessary, treatment
can ensure a longer life for your pet. Don't try cutting overgrown
teeth yourself.

■ Constipation

True constipation is very rare in rabbits. Usually, the reason no stools
are being produced is because the rabbit is not eating, for example,

due to a hairball or malocclusion of the teeth. If no stools have been produced in over 24 hours, then a trip to the veterinarian is called for.

■ Enteritis and diarrhea

Enteritis (inflammation of the bowel) and diarrhea can be due to bacterial infection, occasionally worms, protozoal parasites (coccidiosis), or other causes. Coccidiosis is a common cause and occurs generally where standards of hygiene (overcrowding, inadequate cleaning out, etc.) have fallen. The most common cause is the overgrowth of an abnormal bacterial flora brought on by dietary indiscretion resulting in toxin production, gas production, and often death. Careful dietary management and prompt veterinary care may be lifesaving.

■ **Tyzzer's disease,** caused by a bacterium (*Bacillus piliformis*), affects rabbits, hamsters, gerbils, rats, and mice and is frequently fatal. Diarrhea and loss of appetite are symptoms, or, in the chronic form, steady loss of weight. Prompt treatment with tetracycline antibiotics can alleviate but not necessarily eradicate it.

Rabbits with diarrhea

■ Do not restrict liquid intake

■ As a first aid measure, substitute cold camomile tea for the drinking water

■ Keep the patient warm

■ Seek veterinary care quickly, as diarrhea can often be an indication of serious life-threatening illness

■ Precise diagnosis usually involves sending samples of droppings to the laboratory and hospitalization of your pet

■ If your pet dies, remember that a postmortem examination by the veterinarian will give valuable information, particularly where any other animals may be at risk

■ Salmonella infection

Often from rodent-contaminated food or bedding or contact with animals carrying the bacteria (perhaps without symptoms), this does occur sometimes. It can result in death, particularly in young rabbits. Diarrhea and dullness may be the only symptoms of salmonellosis in pet rabbits.

■ Mucoid enteritis

This is another common cause of diarrhea. It usually combines diarrhea with severe emaciation, but is not well understood and may be due to a number of factors. It affects rabbits of all ages, ending fatally in most unweaned animals and occasionally in adults.

Treatment This depends on correct diagnosis of the type of diarrhea. There is no sure treatment for mucoid enteritis. Other forms require antiparasitic, anticoccidial, or antibiotic drugs.

■ Snuffles

If your pet looks as if it has a chronic cold, it may be the common ailment called snuffles. In its most acute form, this disease may show little beyond a nasal discharge, fever, and fairly rapid death due to

**Above:
Overgrown
rabbit's claws**

**Above: Correctly
trimmed claws**

Overgrown claws

If a rabbit's claws become overgrown, the excess nails can be trimmed off. This is best done by a veterinarian, especially in dark-colored rabbits with dark nails. If you feel competent to trim a pale-colored rabbit's overgrown claws, use animal nail clippers, which are obtainable from pet stores – they are much better than human-type clippers.

You should be able to see the pink core, or "quick," of the claw through the translucent shell. This is where the blood vessels and nerves run. Cut at least 1 cm/^{1}/2 in in front of the tip of the quick.

Temperature

You can check the temperature of your pet by the insertion of a stubby-ended clinical thermometer into the rectum. The normal temperature of a healthy rabbit is between 38.6°C/101.5°F and 40.1°C/104.2°F (much higher than in a human) with an average of 39.4°C/103°F. Remember that excitement and handling may produce a rise in temperature. Do not use a glass thermometer as it may break inside the rabbit if it struggles.

pneumonia. The mild form exhibits sneezing and eye discharge, with no loss of function. The cause is a bacteria called *Pasteurella multocida*.

Treatment Your veterinarian will use a broad-spectrum antibiotic (one antibiotic, lincomycin, is toxic for rabbits and cannot be used) and may, in chronic cases, prescribe eyedrops. Don't delay in seeking professional help; you may avoid having your rabbit progress to pneumonia. Keep the patient warm.

■ Skin disease

Apart from some lumps and bumps (see page 111), there are several specific skin complaints of rabbits including rabbit syphilis. This disease is not infectious for humans or other animals and is common in domestic rabbits. It takes the form of weeping sores around the genital area, on the lips, eyelids, and nose. Severe ulceration can obstruct the passage of urine and droppings and if the germ spreads to internal organs, the rabbit may die. The bacterium that causes rabbit syphilis is similar to the one that causes syphilis in humans and it responds to injections of penicillin or other antisyphilitic drugs.

■ **Ringworm,** mange, various kinds of bacteria, and a pox virus infection can also attack the coat of a rabbit. All need diagnosis by the veterinarian, who may take samples for laboratory tests, and there are specific treatments for each kind. Ringworm usually comes from rats and mice, so make sure your hutches and runs are rodent-proof. It can often be treated by drugs added to the rabbit's food.

■ **Loss of hair and "wet eczema"** of the skin on the undersurface of the hind legs, particularly beneath the hocks, or under the belly of the rabbit is often caused by bad flooring (wire mesh) or lack of sufficient fresh litter on damp, dirty solid floors. Bacteria enter skin abrasions and nasty infections result. Rabbits housed or exercised outdoors are susceptible to fly strike and maggot infestation, which can be serious. Improved housing and management are keys to a cure.

Treatment Antibiotic and antiseptic creams and dressings assist healing.

■ **Ear canker,** caused by a rabbit ear mite, is the most common form of mange in the rabbit. Brown flakes and scabs build up inside the ear and cause the rabbit to scratch the ear with the hind feet.

■ **Prevention** Cleaning the ears regularly (once monthly) with cotton

Fleas

Occasionally, rabbits, particularly those kept outdoors and in warm weather, can become infested with fleas. These parasites cause irritation and scratching. Usually there are telltale signs of fine black coal dust (actually the dried droppings of fleas) on the skin when the hair is parted.

Treatment is with insecticidal sprays or powders of the kind suitable for cats. Because the fleas' eggs fall off the rabbit's body and lie in the bedding and cracks in the hutch floor, sometimes for many months before hatching, the animal's housing should be cleaned thoroughly and treated with a special aerosol that destroys flea larvae in the environment and is effective for several months. This is available from your veterinarian.

swabs dampened in warm olive oil helps ear hygiene. If the condition is present, your veterinarian will prescribe the proper treatment.

■ **Manges** are caused by tiny mites that damage the skin. They are easily killed by modern antiparasitic preparations, but wherever skin disease is diagnosed, you must isolate the patient from other rabbits and clean and disinfect the hutch and run thoroughly.

Treatment The veterinarian may give you some form of medicated bath with which to treat your rabbit if the body is affected. There is no harm in bathing a rabbit provided you use warm water and then dry your pet thoroughly with a soft towel and/or a hair-dryer. For localized problems, special sprays are sometimes used. Drops are used in the ears.

■ **Lumps and bumps** If your rabbit develops one or more bumps under the skin, don't panic about myxomatosis. Other things are far more likely to be the cause of the bumps. Sometimes a swelling will come up on the jaw or there may be several distributed irregularly over the rabbit's head and body. Often there is no loss of appetite, at least at first, and the general condition of the animal seems normal. Abscesses, caused by various types of bacteria that arrive either through the bloodstream or via a bite wound, are commonly the cause. Occasionally, lumps are tumors. However, most are operable if caught early.

Note: All bumps need veterinary attention. Some may need lancing or removal under local anesthetic or ethyl chloride, and usually the veterinarian will also give an injection of an appropriate antibiotic. Seek advice early.

■ Miscellaneous ailments

■ Middle ear disease

If a rabbit starts to tilt its head to one side and, later, develops a tendency to move in circles, it may have an infection of the middle ear. This disease is normally associated with a recent attack of "snuffles," perhaps one as mild as merely a runny nose and watery eyes. The Pasteurella bacterium is the usual cause, and treatment may have to be a prolonged course of broad-spectrum antibiotics. Chronic cases, particularly where the inner ear is also affected, can be very difficult to resolve.

■ Eye problems

The most common eye troubles are runny, with a discharge, perhaps bloodshot eyes on one or both sides. The cause may be a mild injury, a fly-borne infection, or the presence of snuffles.

Treatment Wash the eye carefully with warm saline available from the drugstore, wiping away any crusting around the eyelids. If the condition persists for more than 48 hours or appears to be getting worse, consult your veterinarian. Antibiotic eye preparations may be indicated.

■ Mastitis inflammation

This, with swelling and tenderness of a doe's breast tissue, usually

Less common diseases

There are numerous other, though generally less common, diseases of rabbits. Even appendicitis can occur, the rabbit being one of the few animals other than humans to have an appendix.

■ Within the last ten years, another new disease of rabbits, rabbit hemorrhagic virus or rabbit calicivirus, has spread from China into Europe and Central America. Again, domestic rabbits in contact directly or indirectly with wild rabbits are at risk. The good news is that a protective vaccine is available against this plague that can kill rabbits in as little as two days.

indicates the presence of mastitis. It tends to occur where management is lax and when the offspring are suddenly weaned or removed at, say, three to four weeks rather than the usual seven to eight weeks.

Treatment Bathe the swollen breasts frequently with warm water and seek veterinary attention. Broad-spectrum antibiotics are usually required.

■ Paralysis

Loss of function, paralysis, of the hind parts can be due to violent struggling during handling or some other form of injury. It is a very serious condition needing immediate veterinary attention which usually includes X-raying. Medical treatment is helpful in a minority of cases, but if there is not the first evidence of significant improvement within three weeks of onset, the outlook is bleak.

■ Summary

If you purchase good stock, provide good housing, maintain a regular cleaning routine, and feed your pet an adequate balanced diet, you will find your visits to the veterinarian will be far fewer.

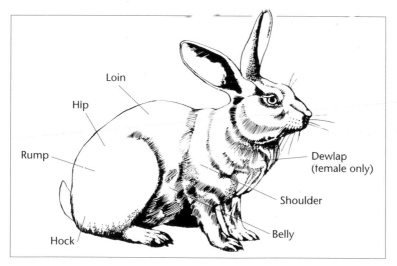

Loin

Hip

Rump

Hock

Dewlap
(female only)

Shoulder

Belly

Guinea pigs

Guinea pigs fall ill from time to time, particularly if overcrowded or kept in unhygienic conditions. Germs and parasites build up in the environment and the result is outbreaks of diarrhea, pneumonia, colds, weakness, and weight loss, sometimes rapidly fatal. Food and bedding contaminated by the urine and droppings of wild rodents may bring in serious infections such as salmonellosis.

■ Seek veterinary help

If a guinea pig falls ill, take it to the veterinarian promptly; diagnosis, sometimes aided by laboratory tests, will be followed by treatment either by injection or by the prescription of drugs to be given orally. The veterinarian won't normally use penicillin on guinea pigs; curiously, it is poisonous for these creatures. Other antibiotics thought to be dangerous for guinea pigs are bacitracin, ampicillin, streptomycin, lincomycin, erythromycin, and tetracycline.

■ Teeth problems
As for rabbits
(see page 106).

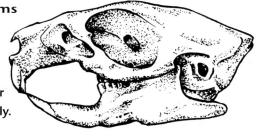

A guinea pig's incisor teeth grow constantly.

✚ Overgrown claws

Trimming a guinea pig's overgrown claws is best done by a veterinarian. However, if you feel competent to perform this task, refer to page 108 and follow the same procedure as for rabbits.

Fleas

Very occasionally, guinea pigs do get fleas. If you suspect that your animal is infested, turn to page 110 and treat as for rabbits.

■ Diarrhea

Similar diseases to those in rabbits (see page 107) occur in guinea pigs. Also, they have a tendency to develop pseudotuberculosis, a bacterial disease that often produces diarrhea and weight loss with death after two to four weeks. An acute form that leads to blood poisoning and death within one to two days also exists. Such cases require urgent veterinary consultation. Diarrhea in guinea pigs is also sometimes due to diet changes or environmental stress; certain antibiotics can cause diarrhea and a fatal enteritis in these animals.

■ Skin disease

This is commonly caused by lice or mites and can be controled by insecticide sprays or powders obtained from the pet store, together with disposal of all bedding and disinfection of the animals' living quarters. Stubborn skin disease may be due to other causes, such as fungus, and needs veterinary attention.

■ Guinea pigs sometimes chew the hair off themselves or one another ("barbering"). In such cases, it can help to change the housing or, at least, the bedding materials. Baldness is commonly seen in heavily pregnant sows – the cause is not known but the hair normally grows back after they give birth.

■ Feet

As in rabbits, rough, damp, or dirty flooring can result in guinea pigs' feet becoming inflamed and even ulcerated. Softer bedding and a change of flooring is indicated, but take the animal to a veterinarian who may treat the sore feet with antibiotics and corticosteroids. Healing often takes a very long time.

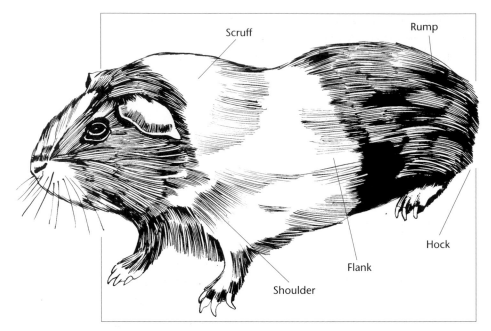

Scruff

Rump

Hock

Flank

Shoulder

■ Lumps and bumps

Many of these that you come across in or under the skin are often abscesses or infected lymph nodes (glands). They require veterinary treatment as for rabbits (see page 111).

■ Other ailments

Problems during pregnancy, and difficult births, which sometimes terminate in death during labor, are quite common. Try to avoid waiting any longer than when the sow is four months old to mate her for the first time (see page 87). Problems during pregnancy are often the result of feeding hay of poor quality. Plenty of roughage in the form of top-quality hay is absolutely essential.

■ Pregnancy toxemia

This disease develops during the last one to two weeks of pregnancy or the first five days after giving birth. The sow is off her food, depressed, and may breathe heavily. Fat animals are more susceptible so avoid overfeeding. This disease progresses rapidly, is difficult to treat, and frequently ends in death. Veterinary attention at the first sign of trouble is essential.

■ Mastitis
As for rabbits (see page 112).

■ Eye problems
As for rabbits (see page 112).

■ Vitamin C deficiency (scurvy)
Guinea pigs need lots of vitamin C regularly. If they don't get enough, they lose weight and fitness, their limb joints become enlarged and painful (due to internal hemorrhages), they are weak and lame, and eventually they die. Symptoms can occur as early as two weeks after a shortage of vitamin C begins.

Treatment Giving 100 mg vitamin C (ascorbic acid) by drops into the mouth once a day and providing fresh vegetables.

Causes of disease

■ The major group of illnesses in guinea pigs is caused by dietary faults. Shortage of good hay can produce "barbering," death of youngsters, loss of condition, overgrowth of teeth with difficulties in eating, and self-mutilation. Poorly balanced diets may lead to bone disease. Moldy vegetable food may produce serious liver damage, enteritis, and a high mortality rate. Lack of fresh vegetables high in vitamin C can lead to scurvy.

■ If one among a group of animals dies, it is wise to have a postmortem examination carried out. Accurate diagnosis enables you to take swift action, perhaps by adding drugs to the water or food, to protect the living.

Hamsters

Hamsters are tougher and less often ill than other domesticated rodents, but they have their special problems.

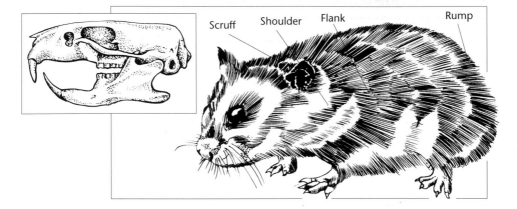

Scruff   Shoulder   Flank   Rump

■ The mouth

■ **Teeth problems** can occur as with rabbits (see page 106). Overgrown teeth, caused usually by the diet not demanding sufficient chewing, may need clipping and filing back by a veterinarian. Feeding too many sweet treats and household tidbits can, as in children, lead to caries (cavities) in the teeth.

Abscesses of the cheek pouches can occur in hamsters due to abrasions caused by sharp food or bedding. Veterinary treatment is necessary.

■ Stomach problems

Diarrhea can be caused by a variety of germs and other factors.
■ Contamination of food or bedding with germs of the ubiquitous Salmonella group is a constant risk to hamsters. The most common source of these bugs is wild mouse or rat droppings. Symptoms may be vague: dullness, lack of appetite, and diarrhea. Death may ensue quickly. Only speedy treatment by a veterinarian, who will inject a tiny quantity of a special antibiotic into the hamster, can save the

day. Certain antibiotics are thought to be toxic to hamsters. They include penicillin, streptomycin, lincomycin, and erythromycin.

■ Wet tail

The nuisance disease of hamsters is undoubtedly "wet tail." This persistent and weakening diarrhea is due to a gastrointestinal upset whose causes seem to be complex. Too much fat in the diet, vitamin deficiency (particularly of the vitamin B group), stress, and several kinds of bacteria have all been blamed at different times.

Treatment This involves improving the animal's eating habits and living conditions, and often, under veterinary advice, putting an antibiotic, such as soluble neomycin, in the hamster's drinking water.

■ Tyzzer's disease

This may also affect hamsters (see rabbits, page 107).

■ Constipation

This is often seen in young hamsters who are just beginning to wean and where only dry food is available. They must be able to reach a supply of water at all times. Constipated hamsters are miserable, exhibit swollen abdomens, and frequently bulging anuses. Consult your veterinarian for treatment.

■ Coughs, sneezes, and snuffles

Hamsters can pick up some of the cold-sore throat viruses of humans, so don't let those afflicted in this way handle or come near your pets. Virus infections contracted from humans can progress to pneumonia and may prove fatal.

Treatment Sneezing, snuffles, and sore noses in hamsters are signs of respiratory infection. As with humans, good nursing may be all that is required – warmth, swabbing away nasal discharges, vitamin supplements, etc. In more severe cases, a veterinarian may prescribe an antibiotic to ward off potentially dangerous secondary infections by bacteria such as Pasteurella.

■ Skin disease

This can be due to fungus (ringworm), mites (mange), infection of bite wounds, or degeneration due to old age. Often, owners mistake two patches of dark coarse hair, one on each side over the hips, for skin disease. Actually, these patches, more obvious in males than in females, are normal and are the sites of special glands. These glands play a part in sexual attraction (hamsters in the wild seek out their mates by smell) and are possibly also used for marking territory.

Diagnosis and treatment The veterinarian will diagnose the type of any skin ailment, often with the aid of laboratory tests on skin or hair scrapings, and then prescribe specific treatment.

Other ailments

■ "Cage paralysis," where a hamster seems to become very weak on its legs, is due to lack of space and exercise. The owner must speedily provide both, not least by installing a good exercise wheel.

■ Pregnancy toxemia can occur as in guinea pigs (see page 116).

■ Diabetes of hereditary origin, where an animal drinks copiously, is sometimes detected by the veterinarian. Such a patient may lose much weight or, alternatively, be obese.

■ Tumors, particularly inoperable ones of the adrenal gland, are found in around 50 percent of hamsters over two years of age.

Note: Besides the above-mentioned antibiotics, certain other chemicals are toxic for hamsters. Among them are DDT and organophosphorous compounds (used in some insecticides and parasiticides).

■ Gerbils

■ Teeth problems

Like the other small pets, gerbils may have to have their front teeth trimmed back if they overgrow. The cause of such exuberant growth is deformities of the mouth structures or, more commonly, nothing to gnaw on in their cage. It should be noted that in all small rodents, the lower incisors are normally approximately three times the length of the uppers and do not require trimming at this length.

■ Diarrhea

The most serious disease of gerbils, often, but not always, causing diarrhea, along with depression, lack of appetite, and weight loss, is Tyzzer's disease (see rabbits, page 107). Sometimes it attacks so ferociously that the victims are suddenly found dead. This disease may prove rapidly fatal (within two days of the onset of symptoms) in up to 70 percent of cases. Treatment is difficult and depends on rapid veterinary attention, fluid therapy, good nursing and the use of

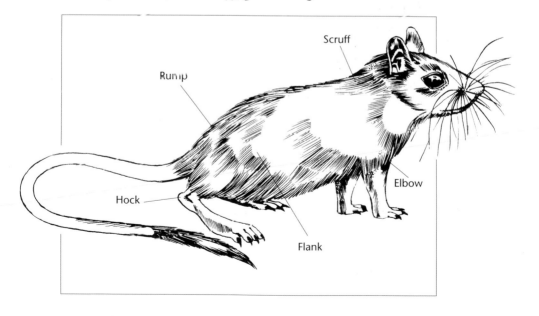

Scruff

Rump

Elbow

Hock

Flank

antibiotics such as oxytetracycline and neomycin.

Diarrhea in gerbils can often be the result of poor feeding, particularly spoiled or stale food or an excess of wet greens. To avoid this, make sure you feed your pet correctly (see page 77).

■ Colds

Sneezes, snuffles, and sore eyes may be the result of streptococcal bacteria picked up from children. Antibiotics are the best treatment.

■ Skin disease

Nasal dermatitis, inflammation of the nose, occurs in five percent of gerbils due to a failure to spread the irritating Harderian gland secretions during grooming. Allowing dust-bathing will help.

■ Other ailments

■ Infected sebaceous gland

The large sebaceous gland located under the belly of gerbils may become infected, inflamed, and swollen. The veterinarian will prescribe a suitable antibiotic/corticosteroid ointment.

■ **Tumors,** some of which are operable, are common in gerbils. The most common organs to be affected are the ovaries and uterus.

■ **Note:** Some narrow-spectrum antibiotics, such as penicillin and streptomycin, can cause dangerous side-effects in gerbils. Only broad-spectrum antibiotics, such as chloramphenicol, tetracyclines, and cephalosporins, will be prescribed for them by the veterinarian.

Rats and mice

If you clean out your pets' cages conscientiously and provide wholesome food and clean water regularly, illness should rarely be seen. Rodents can be affected by a large number of ailments, but these are most often encountered in the large colonies kept by laboratories. If your pet does become ill, take it to your veterinarian, who can give minute injections if necessary or prescribe medicine to be added to the water bottle.

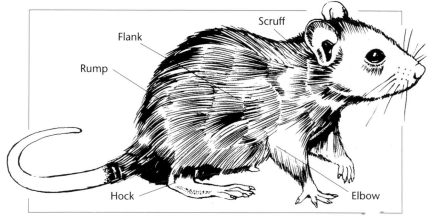

Scruff

Flank

Rump

Hock

Elbow

■ Teeth problems

As with the other small rodents, overgrowth of the gnawing incisor teeth may result in poor appetite and loss of weight. If it occurs, you can carefully trim back the teeth to their normal length using nail clippers. Remember the one to three ratio of upper to lower teeth length (see page 121).

■ Stomach upsets

All the causes described for rabbits and the other rodents can produce diarrhea and digestive upsets in rats and mice, including Tyzzer's disease.

■ **Parasitic worms,** both tapeworms and roundworms, occasionally cause diarrhea, loss of fitness, loss of weight, and, less frequently, rectal prolapse. The presence of worms is easily confirmed by laboratory testing of droppings, and treatment consists of the administration of safe drugs such as mebendazole in food or water.

■ Chest problems

Colds, heavy breathing, wheezing, and runny noses, often accompanied by weight loss and dullness, are signs of respiratory disease – probably the most common type of sickness in rats and mice. Although viruses and bacteria of many kinds are the causal agents of the disease, other factors such as poor housing, bad hygiene, and overcrowding play an important part in predisposing the animals to germ attack. Antibiotics in the water supply may be used to treat such conditions, but prevention in the form of improved housing and management is the watchword.

■ Skin disease

The diseases of the skin affecting rats and mice are those described in the rabbit (page 109) and other small pets.
■ **Skin abscesses** caused by bites when fighting are often seen. Don't keep male mice together – they are likely to do battle.

■ Other ailments

Diseases of the nervous system are common in rats and mice but are not treatable and are mainly of interest only to laboratory scientists. Certain antibiotics, such as penicillin and streptomycin, can be toxic to rats and mice. Your veterinarian has others that can be used safely.

■ Tumors, especially of the breast tissue, are sometimes seen in these animals. In rats they are usually benign, whereas in mice they tend to be malignant. It is feasible for a veterinarian to operate, under general anesthetic, and remove the benign type of tumor.

✚ First aid for the small pet

Small pets need expert attention in most cases when they fall ill
or have an accident. Disease can proceed rapidly, sometimes to
a fatal conclusion, and you should never waste time on patent
remedies and experiments. In general, owners can do far less
for the small pet in trouble than for bigger animals such as cats
and dogs. Diagnosis and advice from your veterinarian must
always be sought without delay.

■ Fractures

Where it is suspected that fractures may have been caused by
a fall or other trauma, do not attempt to splint the animal's
legs with matchsticks or the like. Manipulating the delicate
limbs can easily cause further serious damage to fine nerves
and blood vessels. Instead, pick the animal up by its scruff
(see pages 41–43), wrap it gently in some soft material, keep
it warm, and take it to your veterinarian immediately. Do not
feed the animal as it may have to be anesthetized to prevent
further pain while the limb is splinted or pinned.

■ Small cuts and wounds

These can be bathed gently in warm water and very weak
antiseptic, and then dried. A tiny amount of antiseptic or
antibiotic cream can then be applied to the cut or wound.
However, powders are best avoided on hairy parts of the body
as they tend to create matting.

Vacations

What should you do when you go away? Of course, you must NEVER even contemplate simply piling a vast quantity of food and water into the animal's quarters and hoping it will work its way through them and even have some left over by the time you return.

■ The best thing you can do is to arrange for a friend to visit the house at least once a day to feed and water your pets, and, as necessary, clean them out.

■ Written instructions should be left and are better than verbal ones that can be forgotten easily.

■ Another way is to board out your pet, preferably together with its own familiar accommodations, at a friend's house or at a pet store, boarding kennels (some of these are prepared to board small pets nowadays), or veterinary clinics.

■ Again, make sure that you provide some notes on the animal's usual diet and some of its brand of food, so that the risk of nutritional upset is minimized.

Summary

So now we come to the end of this little instruction manual for owners of small pets. Good luck with your small-pet-keeping, but please, if you are unable to devote regular time and care to the servicing and maintenance of your pet, stick to whatever your particular hobby may be. Only good owners are welcome in this club!

Index